THE MANUFACTURE OF LIQUORS
AND PRESERVES

NOYES PRESS SERIES IN HISTORY OF TECHNOLOGY

The books published in the History of Technology Series are reprints of important works published in the eighteenth and nineteenth centuries. Most of them are of American origin, however some were published in Great Britain, or are early translations of European works.

In addition to describing historical technological devices and processes, many of the books give an insight into the relationship of early technology to the culture of the day.

THE MANUFACTURE OF
LIQUORS AND PRESERVES

History of Technology Vol. No. 3

J. De Brevans

NOYES PRESS
Noyes Building
Park Ridge, New Jersey 07656, U.S.A.

A Noyes Press Reprint Edition

This edition of THE MANUFACTURE OF LIQUORS
AND PRESERVES is an unabridged republication of
the U.S. edition of a French work published in 1893
by Munn & Co.

FOREWORD
1972

This work was well known in France during the nineteenth century. The translation into English by Munn & Co. in 1893 gave an insight into French manufacturing of liquors and preserves that was lacking prior to that time. The great value of the book consists in the formulas, which are so arranged that, if the manufacturer has no distilling plant, he can still produce many of the liquors from the essences.

The first part of the book discusses both alcohol and natural liquors. Processes for distillation, purification and rectification of alcohol are included. The manufacture of natural liquors such as natural and artificial branches, rums, and tafia, are illustrated.

The second and largest part discusses artificial liquors with many formulas. Included are descriptions of the laboratory and plant, and discussions of raw materials, alcohol, essences, spirits, tinctures, distilled waters, juices, syrups, coloring matters, etc.

The third part discusses preserves, including preparation of brandied and preserved fruit.

The fourth part discusses analysis of liquors, and their examination for adulteration.

The Preface was written by Ch. Girard, Director of the Municipal Laboratory of Paris.

THE MANUFACTURE

OF

LIQUORS AND PRESERVES.

TRANSLATED FROM THE FRENCH

OF

J. DE BREVANS,

Chief Chemist of the Municipal Laboratory of Paris.

WITH SIXTY-FIVE ILLUSTRATIONS.

Entered at Stationers' Hall.

New York:
MUNN & CO.
1893.

MACGOWAN & SLIPPER, PRINTERS,
30 BEEKMAN STREET, NEW YORK, N. Y.,
U. S. A.

PREFACE.

A CLEAR and precise manual for the distiller and liquor manufacturer has long been needed in France—a book which by its scope, form and price would be within the reach of all, but nevertheless would be complete enough to give a true picture of the recent discoveries and the true state of the art in this important branch of our national industry. This want has been filled by " The Manufacture of Liquors and Preserves." M. De Brevans, in writing the book, which we have the pleasure of presenting to the public, has accomplished a great service to manufacturers, chemists, etc.

The first part comprises the study of liquors, that is to say, alcohol and natural liquors (brandy, rum, tafia). M. De Brevans says that there is rum which has never seen the Antilles and *kirsch* to which the cherry is a perfect stranger, both being spirituous mixtures made by mixing various chemicals and pharmaceutical products—an art which our neighbors beyond the Rhine have fully mastered.

In the second part the author studies artificial liquors, some pages being devoted to a description of the laboratory and plant of the distiller, including raw materials, alcohol, essences, spirits, tinctures, distilled waters, juices, sirups, etc., without forgetting the coloring matters.

The third part treats of preserves, including brandied and preserved fruit.

The fourth part deals with the analysis of liquors and their examination for adulterations.

M. De Brevans has limited himself to the study of liquors which can be made openly, and leaves in the shade all the dishonest and dangerous products reprobated both by chemistry and hygiene; but, to compensate for this, he has given us a considerable number of clear formulas, easy of application, which permits the distiller and the liquor manufacturer to make a large variety to satisfy the taste of the consumer.

M. De Brevans has brought to the preparation of this work all the accuracy which I have known him capable of during the seven years that I have been able to appreciate the merits of my young collaborator.

CH. GIRARD,
Director of the Municipal Laboratory of Paris.

Paris, April 25, 1890.

TRANSLATOR'S PREFACE.

THE little work of J. De Brevans is well known in France. The great value of the book consists in the formulas, which are so arranged that, if the manufacturer has no distilling plant, he can still make many of the liquors from the essences. The formulas have been left in the metric, or decimal, system, as this system is gaining ground rapidly and there is every hope of its final adoption by manufacturers as a matter of convenience. The tables in the appendix render changes easy from the metric to the common system, or *vice versâ*.

THE MANUFACTURE

OF

LIQUORS AND PRESERVES

PART I.—LIQUORS.

CHAPTER I.

It is very difficult to define in an accurate manner the substances to which the term liquor has been applied, so numerous are the acceptations of this word; it designates certain chemical and pharmaceutical preparations as well as beverages. For the purposes of this work, let us consider liquors as *alcoholic beverages*, and under this title are included brandy, table liquors and aromatic wines.

We include natural liquors in the first class, which comprises alcoholic beverages prepared by simple distillation of the fermented juices of fruits. The preparation of brandy, kirsch, rum, and other liquors equally well known will be considered first. In the second class are included table liquors, or artificial liquors, as they are sometimes called, which includes beverages in which the base is alcohol or water, and only differ from each other by the presence or absence of sugar and in the nature of the aromatic substances, which are equally used by the perfumer and liquor

manufacturer. In this class of liquors are included
absinthe, anisette, curaçoa, etc. In the third class
are included the aromatic wines, many of which were
known to the ancients. In these wines the alcohol is
not isolated, the base of the beverage being wine, or
the juice of crushed grapes. Among wines of this class
are included vermouth, hydromel, etc.

In addition to liquors proper, many articles, such as
sirups and preserves, are manufactured, not only for
direct consumption, but for use in the manufacture of
the liquors themselves. Under this head will be included the preparation of simple and compound
sirups, brandied fruits, *glacéd* fruit, etc.

The ancients had no knowledge of alcohol proper,
which was only discovered in the thirteenth century,
but they prepared aromatic wines, and the old manu-
scripts transmit a large number of receipts to us. The
most ancient liquor of which we have any knowledge
is hippocras, the invention of which is attributed to
Hippocrates, the celebrated Greek physician; pri-
marily, it is only an infusion of cinnamon in wine
sweetened with honey, but with the change of fashion,
this drink became more complicated and was served
on all great occasions. This drink was given the place
of honor during the middle ages, and it still figured
among the refreshments served at the court of Louis
XIV. and Louis XV. The Romans introduced various
other liquors and aromatic wines, and in the middle
ages people were equally addicted to their use. The
discovery of alcohol made a revolution in the art of
the *liquoriste*, and all the old receipts soon fell into
oblivion. The wine of absinthe of Pliny only remains.
We now call it vermouth.

CHAPTER II.

ALCOHOL.

ALCOHOL is the principal product of fermentation, particularly of glucose, and this includes nearly all the sugar confined in fruits. The transformation of this material into alcohol takes place with the development of a special ferment—alcoholic fermentation, of which one variety is that produced by brewer's yeast. The ferment is represented in Fig. 1. From a chemical point of view, alcohol is a hydrocarbon; that is to say,

FIG. 1.—BREWER'S YEAST.

composed of carbon and the elements of water—oxygen and hydrogen. It is represented chemically by the formula C_2H_6O. It is a limpid liquid, of a density of 0·7939 at a temperature of 15° (C.), when it is perfectly anhydrous, or, as it is termed, absolute. It boils under a pressure of 760 mm. at a temperature of 78·4° (C.) It has never been solidified, but it becomes viscous when exposed to the temperature produced by a mixture of ether, carbonic acid and snow. Its taste is burning and its odor is weak. It forms the active principle of all fermented beverages. It burns freely with a blue flame, giving out much heat, but little light. Alcohol is mixed with water in all proportions, producing a slight warmth. Alcohol is a great solvent for a large number of substances, particularly for essences.

Alcohol was unknown before the twelfth century, in Europe. It is almost certain that the discovery of alcohol is due to the Arabs. We are indebted for this important discovery to a Frenchman, Arnauld de Villeneuve, born in Provence in 1740, who was a celebrated professor of the University of Montpellier. In his works he often speaks of alcohol. In 1813 Arnauld de Villeneuve died, leaving science a pupil worthy of him, Raymond Lulle or Lully. To this chemist is due, in the midst of an adventurous career, many important chemical discoveries in the process of extraction of alcohol, the most important of which was the method of concentration of the "spirit of the wine," which had before been very weak. He can be considered as the inventor of rectification. He wrote many treatises on alcohol, as did also Savonarola, J. B. Porta, J. R. Glauber, and others. In the eighteenth century alcohol became the base of medicines and of liquors for the table. The method of preparation became more scientific and alchemy gave place to chemistry.

SECTION I.—DISTILLATION.

Distillation has for its object the separation of a volatile substance from other substances which are fixed at the highest temperature of ebullition of the volatile substance. For example, in the separation of alcohol from wine or other fermented drink, it is necessary to treat a mixture of alcohol, water and other substances. Alcohol boils under normal conditions at a temperature of 78·5° (C.) and water at 100° (C.) If now the mixture be heated to 78·5° and up to 100°, the alcohol will be volatilized and it can be obtained from the vapor by condensation. At 100° and over the water would begin to boil and give off vapor. The distilling apparatus is termed an alembic in its simplest form. In principle it is a flask which has a long neck communicating with an apparatus for condensing the vapor, usually by a vermicular tube, or worm as it is called. At the right temperature the vapor of the liquid is produced in large quantities and is condensed in the worm. The crude apparatus of J. B. Porta is illustrated in Fig. 2, in which G is the alembic, *t* the worm, C the condenser. Having now

described the alembic in its simplest form, which is
still frequently used in the laboratory for experimental
purposes, we come to a modern still. It consists, Fig.
3, of a still consisting of the alembic and head, 4, connected with the worm, 6, by the swan's neck, 5. This

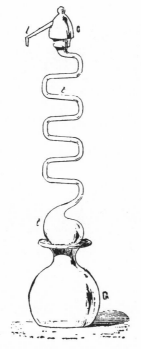

FIG. 2.—DISTILLING APPARATUS OF PORTA.

apparatus has innumerable changes and improve-
ments, the alembic in many cases being sunk in a
water bath instead of being exposed to the naked fire.

The simple still, such as has just been described,
does not permit, at the first distillation, of a liquid

being condensed which is sufficiently strong in alcohol
to be used directly by consumers.   The product of the
first distillation must now be subjected to a redistilla-
tion, which has for its object the elimination of water.

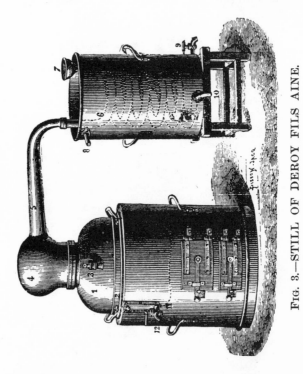

FIG. 3.—STILL OF DEROY FILS AINE.

This occasions a great loss of time and fuel.   To
obviate these difficulties, an apparatus called a wine
heater was devised, which permits of alcohol being
obtained sufficiently concentrated for some purposes
at the first operation.

I.—Distillation of Wine.

The first apparatus constructed to arrive at this object was that of Edouard Adam, who in 1800 thought of the application of the wash bottles of Woulf to distillation. This alembic permitted of the distillation of thirty hektoliters forty liters of wine in six hours.

The somewhat crude apparatus of Adam was modified in 1818 by Derosne, and since by Cail. It consists of two stills placed at different heights. These stills communicate with each other by a curved pipe, designed to carry the vapors of the first furnace to the second. Connected with the second still is a column or tube containing semicircular disks of unequal size placed one above another. In consequence of this arrangement the vapors ascending come in contact with large surfaces moistened with wine. Another rectifier is over this, and the vapors are finally condensed in a worm, the first spirals giving the highest per cent. of alcohol. The worm can be tapped at different points to obtain alcohol of all degrees of strength. The Laugier apparatus (Fig. 4) is on the same principle. It is composed of two stills, A and B, placed at different heights. The first, A, receives the direct heat of the naked fire, the second, B, is heated by the flame and gas of the fire. The vapors produced by the heating of the wine in A are condensed in the liquid of B, which is thus rendered more alcoholic. The operation in brief is as follows : The liquid intended for distillation flows from the reservoir, E, into the vessel, D, entering its lower part and serving to condense the alcoholic vapor. From this vessel the warm fluid passes by means of the tube, r, into the lower part of the dephlegmator, C, which is heated by the hot vapors evolved from the material in the stills, A and B. In the still, B, the fluid undergoes a rectification, and the vinasse flows by the tube, S, into the first still, A. The hot vapor is carried by the pipe, m, from A to B ; the tube, p, carries the alcoholic vapors into the dephlegmator. The tube, q, conveys the phlegma into the still, B. The tubes from C carry the vapors to the condenser, D. The system seems to be very economical, and is used with great success in the central part of France, where a considerable portion of the wine produced is used in manufacturing alcohol. A large num-

FIG. 4.—APPA

A, first still heated by the fire ; B, second s
D, conde

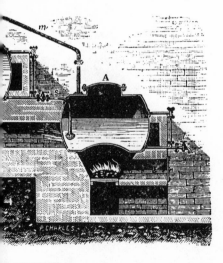

LAUGIER.

smoke, etc.; C, dephlegmation vessel;
voir.

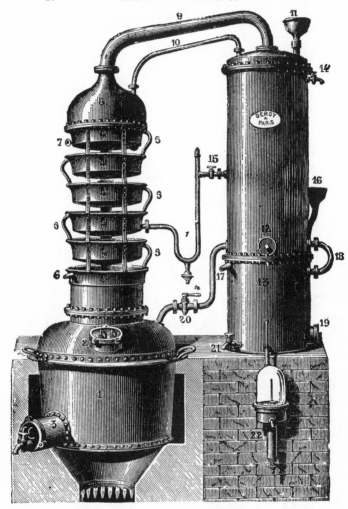

FIG. 5.—APPARATUS WITH LENTICULAR PLATES.

ber of forms of distilling apparatus have been constructed after those of Laugier. Disregarding the various
modifications of this and other systems, let us proceed
directly to the consideration of the most modern forms
of distilling apparatus. Different systems are employed. The ones more generally adopted are those
of Deroy and Egrot.

The Deroy Sons apparatus (Fig. 5) consists of lenticular plates, numbered 4, superimposed on the still.
The still, 1, is charged by pouring wine in at funnel, 11. The condenser, 13, is filled with water, or if
desired, with the wine which is to be operated upon.
The still having been charged and started by the application of heat, a stream of water proportioned to
the required strength of the alcohol descends from
plate, 4, to plate, 4, by the pipes 5 and goes out by the
pipe, 6. The strength of the alcohol can be varied by
the temperature which is maintained in the plates or
cisterns, 4. The vapors pass up from the still and come
in contact with the inner walls of the cisterns, which
are kept cool. The vapors which have arrived at 8
expand and pass through the swan's neck, 9, into the
wine heater, 12, which contains a worm, and from
thence to the condenser, 13, by the pipe, 18, where they
are condensed in the worm and pass out to be tested
by the hydrometer, 22. In this tortuous ascension the
alcoholic vapors can be brought back to the still by
the tube, 15. M. Deroy also makes a similar apparatus
having four reservoirs or cisterns (Fig. 6). This suffices
for wines which are weak in alcohol, but for wines
which are rich in alcohol another cistern is necessary.
The general arrangement is the same as in Fig. 5. The
following description of the Egrot apparatus is taken
from the SCIENTIFIC AMERICAN SUPPLEMENT, No.
448, as the description is given in more detail than in
M. Brevans' book.

The continuous distilling apparatus of Mr. Egrot's
invention are especially applicable to fermented liquids,
molasses and wines. In devising them, the inventor's
object has been to reduce the dimensions of the distilling column, and principally the height thereof, which,
in ordinary apparatus, is considerable.

The result is a diminution in the purchase price and
in the cost of installation and carriage. Such result
has been obtained by increasing the length of the
liquid's circulation in each shelf and by diminishing

the number of shelves. In fact, there are but four or five of the latter in Egrot's column, while there are 18

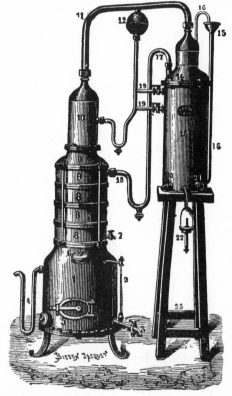

Fig. 6.—APPARATUS FOR CONTINUOUS DISTILLATION.

in those of Dubrunfant and Champonnois, and as many as 32 in that of Savalle. From this diminution

in the number of shelves or trays results a diminution
of pressure in the column, and, consequently, more
regularity in the work, a better product, and less prim-
ing.   At the same time, the total surface being less,
the external cooling is not so great.

The Egrot distilling apparatus (Fig. 7) consists of an
alembic, of a wine heater, and of a condenser.   The

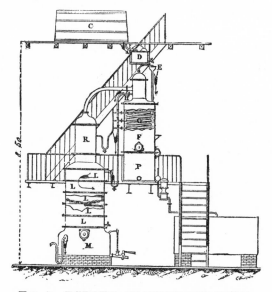

FIG. 7.—EGROT'S STATIONARY STILL.

alembic, M, is of small dimension as compared with
the column which it serves to support.   The distilling
column, which is in five parts, supports another column
of smaller diameter, which contains a certain number
of rectifying shelves.

The wine heater and the condenser, which are both
cylindrical, are traversed by a worm that terminates

at the test apparatus.   Fig. 8 gives the details of the arrangement of a shelf, and shows the course taken by the liquid, which, after entering at A, from the upper shelf, traverses four concentric rings arranged one under another, and makes its exit at E, in the center of the shelf, which latter is also the lowest point of its travel.   From thence a bent tube leads it to the point,

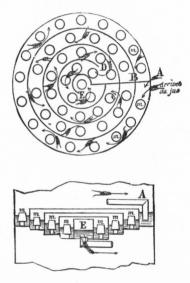

FIG. 8.—PLAN AND SECTION OF ONE OF THE
RECTIFYING SHELVES.

A, of the lower shelf.   The apparatus, in another form, when mounted upon two wheels and drawn by a horse, is very transportable, and is capable of being set in operation immediately upon reaching its destination.

Each shelf or disk is provided with quite a number of tubes, m, of small dimensions, which allow the alco-

holic vapor coming from the alembic to bubble up
through the liquid, and thus have numerous points of
contact therewith. This arrangement likewise allows
the liquid to travel a considerable distance within a
very short time. The apparatus represented (Fig. 7)
is capable of treating 110 gallons per 24 hours.

It is easy to see how the still works. From the reservoir, C, the wine is introduced steadily into the wine
heater, F, through the intermedium of the regulating
cistern, D, where its level is kept constant. There is
thus obtained a uniform discharge from the cock, E.
The wine gradually rises in the heater, F, and becomes
heated in contact with the worm, G, in which the alcoholic vapors are condensing. It afterward enters
the distilling column, L, through the tube, H, and descends from shelf to shelf, and, in doing so, becomes
deprived of more and more of its alcohol by contact
with the vapor that is rising in the column. When the
wine reaches the alembic it is entirely freed from alcohol, and the *vinasse* that continuously flows through
the siphon, S, contains not a trace thereof. The alcoholic vapor follows an opposite direction. From the
alembic, M (heat by steam or otherwise), it rises and
traverses each shelf, and becomes richer and richer in
contact with the richer wine that it meets at every
moment.

It afterward traverses the rectifying column, R,
which contains a certain number of shelves, and is then
led by a swan neck to the wine heater, where it is
analyzed. The liquefied portions return to the column
and the others condense in the cooler, P, and when
they make their exit from the latter they go to the test
apparatus.

There are fourteen sizes of these stills, that range in
capacity from 88 to 220 gallons per 24 hours.

In certain cases, Mr. Egrot adds to his apparatus
certain accessory arrangements for special purposes.
Thus, in order to permit of the production of alcohols
of a higher proof than those afforded by ordinary apparatus, he adds a rectifying head, which will give an
alcohol exceeding 85°.

For the manufacture of cordials, the alcoholic vapors,
before entering the condenser, are introduced into a
special receptacle, called an "anising box," in which
are arranged the aromatic materials, such as anise,
absinthe, juniper, etc.

II.—Distillation of Alcohol for Industrial Purposes.

We have seen at the commencement of this chapter the perfected apparatus which serves in the treatment of wines. These stills are the simple common form of apparatus which have for their object the manufacture of alcohols, which at the first distillation shall be as concentrated as possible. But in the industrial arts not only must the alcohol be free from water, but also must be subjected to a process which permits of the elimination of the various odorous alcohols, such as amylic, etc., which are formed at the same time the alcohol, or ethyl alcohol, as it would be well to call it, is distilled. These materials render the product unfit for consumption, not only on account of the odor, but by reason of their toxic qualities. It was therefore necessary to devise some means of obtaining this end.

Alcohol from Beets.—The transformation of beet root sugar into alcohol is made in several ways. The three principal methods are as follows :

1. The extraction of juice by scraping the beet, the expression of the pulp and adding yeast to the sweet liquid. This method is sometimes the only one employed, and tends to become obsolete, on account of the expense of so much hard labor. The beets are washed, scraped, and the pulp is put in sacks and submitted to the pressure of a hydraulic press. The juice is put in barrels where 0·01 or 0·003 of sulphuric acid is added, as well as brewer's yeast, in the proportion of 8 kilogrammes for 150 hektoliters. The vats are maintained at a temperature of 20° C. The fermentation begins at once and continues for six or eight hours.

The fermentation being finished, the distillation is proceeded with as rapidly as possible, so that there will be no alteration in the liquid.

2. Maceration of beets by cutting and straining and fermentation of the juice. By this method, due to M. Champonnois, the greater part of the work is done in the agricultural distilleries. Figs. 9 and 10 are cuts of a distillery by maceration, the beets having been washed and cut and rubbed very fine or cut in slices termed in the trade *cossettes.* These cossettes, after having been moistened with water acidulated with sulphuric acid, 2 liters of acid to 1,000 kilogrammes of beets, are thrown into wooden vats three in each range. These vats can hold at least 250 kilogrammes

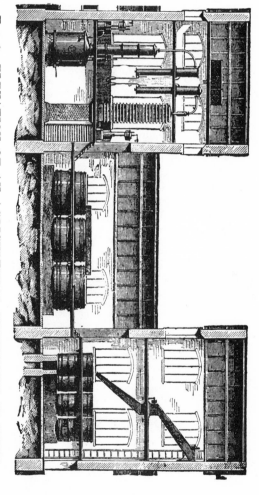

FIG. 9.—ELEVATION OF AN AGRICULTURAL DISTILLERY OF BEET ROOTS WORKING BY MACERATION.

of the prepared beets. These vats have double bottoms of wood or sheet iron perforated by a large number of small holes. We find 200 liters of liquid nearly boiling arising from the previous maceration for 250 kilogrammes of beets. At the end of an hour the liquid in vat No. 1 is passed into vat No. 2, which has been previously charged with a new quantity of material, this second maceration being effected in an hour. The third vat is filled with the beet material, and, by a new charge in 1, its liquid passes into 2 and that of No. 2 into No. 3, and so on. A new charge of beets in No. 1 requires the contents of No. 3 to be drawn off into the fermentation vat. The beet mixture of 1 which is not rich enough is returned to a heater. In the meantime the apparatus is recharged, and, this done, it receives the liquid of No. 3. A new series of operations recommences, changing the order of the vats.

The liquid, on arriving in the fermentation vat, must be subjected to a moderate temperature of 170° C. The vat has now received 250 liters of liquid, 4 kilogrammes of brewer's yeast previously diluted with 6 to 8 liters of the liquid itself, all added gradually. At the end of twenty-four hours this fermentation vat is put into communication with another empty vat, which is divided into two equal parts, and is filled with the juice of fermentation. The simultaneous filling of the two half full vats is continued as the first was, by means of a fine stream of juice. At the end of 12 hours the two vats are filled, and the fermentation can be continued, and at the end of another twelve hours the operation can be considered as terminated. One of the vats is allowed to cool and the contents are distilled 24 hours after, while the other vat, divided in two parts, in its turn serves to start the fermentation of a new quantity of fresh juice, and the operation is continued in the manner already described.

3. Direct fermentation of beets. In this system of Le Play the beets are washed with hot beet liquor and sliced into the forms of ribbons. These pieces are placed one above another, so as to allow the free passage of steam. The beets are put in sacks and sunk in vats with juice which has already been subjected to the fermentation process. In addition to the juice. 0·002 of sulphuric acid is added and the whole is warmed to 20° C., and the fermentation started with yeast. The fermentation which takes

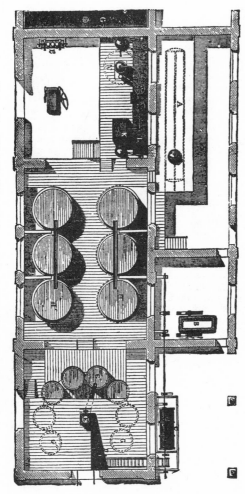

FIG. 10.—PLAN VIEW OF BEET ROOT DISTILLERY.

place in the body of the beet is very intense and works with great rapidity, so that in 12 to 24 hours the transformation of sugar to alcohol is complete. Four charges of beets are used in the same bath, the quantity of yeast being diminished each time. The alcoholic liquid is distilled by special apparatus, which will be described later.

Alcohol from Molasses.—Alcohol is not made to any great extent from molasses in Europe, but the process is largely used in the colonies to make rum. The molasses is freed from water so as to obtain a solution with the density of 1·055 to 1·060, and heated to 23° C. The mass is acidulated by sulphuric acid mixed with brewer's yeast previously diluted. The proportions of these two substances are, 1 kilogramme 500 grammes of sulphuric acid at 66° and as much yeast for 100 kg. of molasses. The fermentation takes place rapidly, and lasts about twenty-four hours. When the fermentation is completed the liquid is saturated with milk of lime, then it is left for twelve hours, after which it is distilled ; 10,000 kilogrammes of molasses give about 2,800 liters of fine alcohol and 1,000 kilogrammes of potassium.

Alcohol from Grain.—The alcoholization of starchy materials is based on the saccharification of this principle by a ferment diastase, or by a dilute acid or on the fermentation of sugar must or wort. Diastase is a soluble ferment which is developed in the germination of grains and which has the property of rendering starch soluble, and by its continued action of transforming it into glucose.

In the manufacture of alcohol diastase is not procured in the pure state. It is prepared from malt. Malt is the germinated grain of barley dried to preserve and arrest the too prolonged action of the diastase on the starch of the grain. Alcohol is obtained by the saccharification of malt of an excellent quality, but, as the price is high, the method using diastase is reserved for the production of brandy from grain. The alcoholization of grains gave the following quantity of grain :

100	kg. of rice give	36	liters pure alcohol
100	" " wheat give	32	" " "
100	" " rye give	28	" " "
100	" " maize give	25	" " "
100	" " barley give	25	" " "
100	" " oats give	22	" " "

Saccharification by Malt.—The malt reduced to pow der is made from the following cereals : Wheat, rye, German wheat, maize ; 25 per cent. of barley malt is sufficient for this operation, which is conducted by a process known as saccharification by hot water. The grains reduced to flour are mixed with a quantity of water heated to 50° or 60° C., which is necessary to obtain a clear paste, and is then thoroughly stirred up. After half an hour sufficient boiling water is gradually added with constant stirring until the temperature is 65° to 70° C. The vat is then covered, and saccharification is completed in two or three hours. If the operation has been successfully carried out, there will now be a saccharine wort including a weight of water equal to four times the weight of the dry materials. This wort is now subjected to a temperature which is most conducive to regular fermentation.

Another method of saccharification is by the aid of steam. This operation has great advantages, as the proportion of water added and the temperature can be regulated at will. The best apparatus is that of M. Lacambre. This apparatus is supplied with a cylinder provided with an agitator. The flour or finely powdered grain is introduced into the cylinder provided with a double bottom, and the agitator is put in motion. At the end of 15 or 20 minutes steam is gradually admitted, until the temperature is raised to 65°, and the mash is stirred continually. This temperature having been obtained, the mash is allowed to rest for half or three-quarters of an hour, when it is agitated anew. This is continued for three or four hours, when, the saccharification being complete, a current of cold water is introduced below the inner bottom, and the wort is cooled until the proper temperature for fermentation is reached.

Saccharification by Acids.— Saccharification by the use of acids, although more economical, has the disadvantage of rendering the malt too solid for cattle food, but it is more expeditious than the preceding processes, and is applicable to the treatment of materials which are not easily attacked by the diastase of malt, among which are maize, rice, etc. Saccharification by acid is conducted as follows : The ground grain is thrown into vats or tubs of water containing 6 per cent. of sulphuric acid at 60°, or 10 per cent. of hydrochloric acid at 22°. The mixture is heated by a coil of pipe containing

steam.   After some hours the material is in the form
of sirup, which is decanted into other vats, where the
free acid is neutralized with chalk; cold water is added
until the temperature is reduced to 22° C.   The sirup
is then sent into the fermentation vats, where it is
mixed with brewer's yeast.

Alcohol from Potatoes.—The alcoholization of potatoes depends on the same principle as that of the
alcoholization of grains, the agent employed being
either malt or an acid, the malt method being that
usually employed.   The potatoes are thoroughly
washed and cooked by steam in a cylindrical heater,
hermetically closed; when the potatoes are still hot,
they are reduced to pulp.   This pulp goes through a
hopper into the saccharification vats, which are already
charged with 6 per cent. of malt diluted with water.
When filled the temperature is raised to 70° or 75° C.,
stir continually for two hours.   The saccharification being completed, the fluid mass is thrown on a
sieve, when it falls into a cooling tank, where it remains until it attains a temperature of 25° C.   It is
then sent into the fermentation vats, where 3 or 4 per
cent. of brewer's yeast is added.   Alcohol obtained
from potatoes is poor, and requires great care in rectifying.

Distilling Apparatus.—The forms of apparatus which
are chiefly employed in distilling grains, etc., are those
of M. Champonnois and M. Savelle.

The apparatus of Savalle (Fig. 11) is composed of a
rectangular iron distilling column, A, formed of a
base and twenty-five closely fitted boxes fastened together, with six bolts at each joint.   B is an arrangement called *brise mousse*, which tends to break up any
froth; C is a tubular wine heater; D is a tubular condenser; E is a hydrometer for testing the strength of
the alcohol.   The heat is graduated by the regulator,
E.   The fermented juice is heated in the wine heater or
by a direct steam coil.   Condensed vapor from the wine
heater, C, is returned to the rectifying column as "low
wines," while the lower condenser, D, takes the lighter
and more volatile product and condenses it.   M. Collette has devised, after years of experiment, a distilling apparatus (Fig. 12) which permits of the treatment of thick mashes as well as the more liquid, and
of the production of alcohol of greater purity and of
a higher degree of spirituosity also with the added ad-

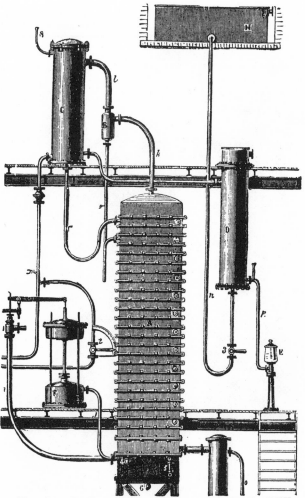

FIG. 11.—SAVALLE'S APPARATUS FOR THE
DISTILLATION OF GRAIN.

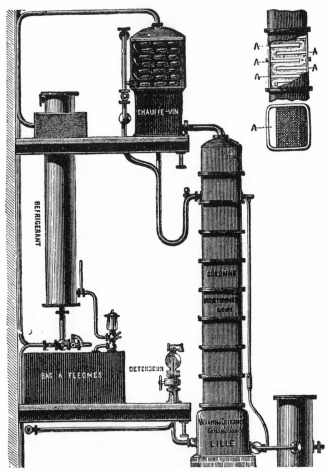

FIG. 12.—DISTILLING COLUMN OF THE COLLETTE
SYSTEM.

vantage that the apparatus takes up less space. According to Maerker, a marked advantage of this apparatus is that the wine, which circulates from plate to plate in the column, is constantly exposed to the rising vapors which, at the end of their tortuous passage, become much enriched. These columns, in the distilleries of MM. Collette, at Allennes, Moers, and Seclin, each treat 20,000 kilos. of maize and 200,000 beets in twenty-four hours. All yeast used in fermentation must be perfectly pure.

SECTION II.—PURIFICATION OF ALCOHOL.

The industrial alcohols which have already been described are obtained by a preliminary distillation in the state of what is called in French *flegmes.* By this name is understood aqueous liquids containing 45° to 75° of alcohol. These flegmes contain other impurities which are more volatile than ethyl alcohol; for example, the aldehydes. To rid the alcohol of these and other impurities is the reason why the alcohol should be rectified. Rectification is dependent upon fractional distillation; that is to say, the separation of liquids by order of their volatility. In the alcohol manufacturer's language, there are five classes of liquids. that they name as follows : 1, poor alcohol ; 2, middling good ; 3, fine alcohol ; 4, extra fine ; 5, absolute alcohol. Two methods are chiefly employed in the purification of alcohol : 1, the physical method, which includes rectification, use of absorbent materials, electricity, etc.; 2, the chemical method, in which substances are employed which have the property of destroying the principal impurities and the disagreeable odor.

Physical Method.—Several years ago the filtration of alcohol through animal black (bone black) was in favor. The price of materials having increased, it was found necessary to abandon the process. In Germany and Sweden they largely employ wood charcoal. The filters are large tubular vessels provided with two bottoms. These filters hold about 150 kilogrammes of charcoal, each filter permitting of the filtration of 60 liters of alcohol at 50° in 24 hours. In the construction and management of these filters the utmost economy must prevail. Fig. 13 represents a battery of filters arranged according to the best practice. Cal-

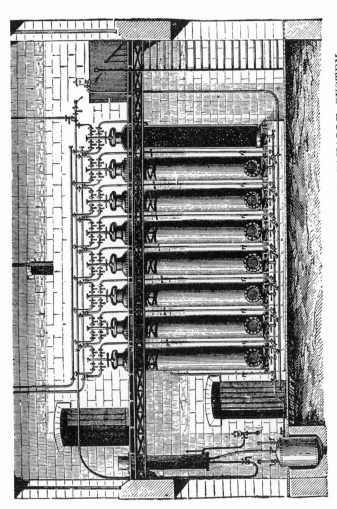

FIG. 13.—BATTERY OF ALCOHOL FILTERS—SAVALLE SYSTEM.

cined charcoal must be used. Unfortunately, charcoal does not possess its remarkable disinfectant qualities for a great length of time and the revivification presents many difficulties, so that it can be only pursued in a country where charcoal is cheap. Oils are very good absorbents of the odorous principles, but their application in regard to alcohol is very limited.

Soap has been equally recommended by M. Kletzinsky, as a deodorizer, etc. For 20 liters of poor alcohol use one kilogramme of Marseilles soap. Alcohol distilled by this method has no odor and is more concentrated than the primitive alcohol, the soap retaining the water. The soap can be used over again by removing the impurities by a current of steam.

Chemical Method.—The chemical substances employed for the purification of alcohol are divided, according to M. Larbaletrier, into four groups.

1. Oxidizing Agents.—The metallic oxides, nitric, chromic, hydrochloric and other acids; the permanganates, the hypochlorites, ozone, oxygen, air, etc.

2. Substances used empirically without explaining their mode of action, such as sulphuric acid and alum.

3. The method of M. L. Naudin, in which, on the liberation of hydrogen, the aldehydes absorb two equivalents of hydrogen, which transforms them into the corresponding alcohols. Alcohols which include a large proportion of aldehyde, ethylic, propylic, butyric, and other compounds are acted upon by the hydrogen produced by electrolysis, which acts upon them, producing ethylic, propylic, butyric and amylic alcohols.

4. Products in which the action is due to certain special properties; for example, the alkalies (potassium, sodium, ammonium), lead acetate, etc.

SECTION III.—RECTIFICATION OF ALCOHOL.

The rectification of alcohol necessitates three series of operations. The first comprises the distillation of alcohol at a temperature of 68° (C.) This first operation gets rid of the ethers and the more volatile alcohols and a part of the aldehydes. The second operation, which is conducted at 68° to 100°, gives a good quality of alcohol, mixed, however, with aldehyde.

From 100° to 102° the remainder of the alcohol distills, which constitutes the third operation. The part lost in this operation is 5 per cent.

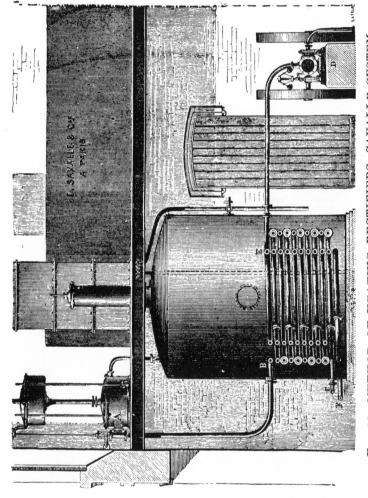

Fig. 14.—METHOD OF HEATING RECTIFIERS—SAVALLE SYSTEM.

Apparatus for Rectifying.—The apparatus generally employed (in France) is that of M. Savalle and of M. Deroy. There are two systems employed by M. Savalle. The one necessitates the application of water for cooling the condenser, and in the other this operation is performed by a current of air. The exhaust steam of an engine is used in this apparatus to heat the still (Fig. 14). This steam is conducted in coils around the inner portion of the still. A regulator governs the temperature and allows the proper temperature for distillation to be maintained. Two hundred thousand liters of alcohol a day can be rectified in this machine, as it is of very large size.

The apparatus is put in operation by charging the still with the alcohol at 40° to 50°. Steam is then admitted into the serpentine coil of pipe. The liquid heats slowly and the vapors rise through the column, which gradually becomes heated, to the tubular condenser, when water is admitted and the vapors are condensed.

The Savalle apparatus for rectifying alcohol by using air to condense the vapors is represented in Fig. 15. It consists of a still, A, which receives the alcoholic liquor at 45°. In the interior is a steam coil. B is the rectifying column; C and D being condensers. The least volatile vapors are condensed in C. The vapors which are not condensed in C pass into the refrigerator, D, where they are condensed. The still is filled with alcohol to be rectified and the alcohol is poured on the plates. By this means the column is washed and freed from the empyreumatic products of the preceding rectification, and, when the operation is started again, the plates will be charged with alcohol of great strength. This proceeding is economical of fuel. The apparatus being started, the alcoholic vapors rise and are condensed little by little on the plates. This liquid emits in its turn vapors containing very little water, which escape from the column and are analyzed in the condenser, which is formed of a tubulous cylinder, the tubes of which serve for a passage of a current of air which replaces the water. The pure alcoholic vapors which traverse the condenser then go to the second condenser or refrigerator, while the aqueous vapors which are condensed are returned to the column. The second condenser or refrigerator works equally well with air. The apparatus of MM. Deroy is composed (Fig.

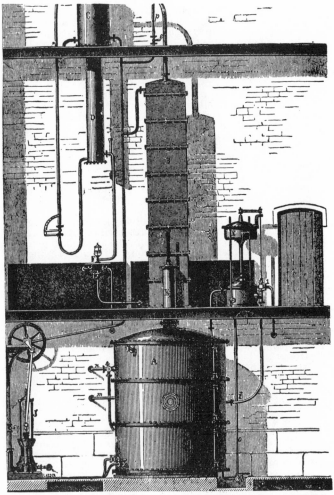

FIG. 15.—SAVALLE APPARATUS FOR RECTIFYING.

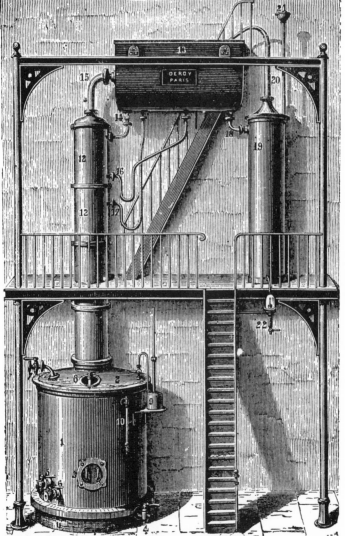

DEROY
PARIS

FIG. 16.—DEROY FILS AINE SYSTEM OF RECTIFYING.

16) of four parts, the heater, or still, the column, the condenser and refrigerator. The heating is generally done by steam, as it must be gradual. The more volatile portions commence to pass over at 78°, while the alcohol does not really begin to distill until 80° are reached. The vapors rise in the column, where they encounter the plates, which arrest the least volatile portion, while the lighter portion is condensed or a second separation takes place, until the alcohol arrives at the refrigerator. Meanwhile the product of the latest portion of the vapors requires another separation, because the vapors condensed immediately after the ethers have not acquired the fineness necessary for the first quality, their strength being rarely 92°, while the best should be 95°. For a second operation the heat is withdrawn and the entire apparatus is thoroughly cleaned.

CHAPTER III.

Natural Liquors.

SECTION I.—BRANDY FROM WINE.

Cognacs.—Under the name of cognac are comprised six kinds of liquors, known in commerce under the following names :

1. *La Grande Champagne.* (Fine champagne.)—These are the cognacs or brandies most highly esteemed. They are distilled in 29 communes of Charente (department). The center of the manufacture is Segonzac, which fixes the market price on the first day of each month. The average production of this brandy is 115,000 hectoliters, at a strength of 70°.

2. *La Petite Champagne.*—This region comprises 50 communes, of which the center and principal market is Châteauneuf.

3. *Les Borderies ou Premiere Bois.*—Under this name are comprised the brandy from 90 communes, which produced 200,000 hectoliters before the advent of the phylloxera. The principal centers are Cognac, Hiersac, Jarnac, Matha, Angoulême, Barbezieux, Jonzac Pons, Saintes.

4. *Les Deuxièmes Bois ou Bous Bois.*—The center of the production of this variety is Rouillac and St. Jean d'Angely.

5. *Saintonage.*—This is brandy produced at the border of the department of Gironde from Mortagne to Rochelle. The most estimable varieties prove to be those vines planted in the interior, as the grapes grown along the shore have a very pronounced taste of the soil.

6. *Rochelle.*—Under this name are included all the brandies produced from vines planted near the sea in a salt, marshy soil. This produces a pronounced taste which improves with age. The center of the manufacture is La Rochelle.

The distillation is made in the winter following the vintage. The product is superior to that obtained by using a wine a year old. The stills used have a capacity of 100 to 500 liters. The apparatus for using the open fire is very crude (Fig. 17). To start the process the alembic or still and the wine heater are filled with wine ; 300 liters of wine in each. By careful distillation 120 liters of liquid can be obtained, which is called the *premier brouillis.* This wine, which is exhausted, is replaced by wine from the wine heater, which is filled anew. The distillate which is obtained is called the *deuxième brouillis.* A third operation with the same conditions gives what is called the *troisième brouillis.*

FIG. 17.—BRANDY STILL.

After the third operation the wine heater is filled with the distilled liquid which has been collected. This is distilled and the *quatrième brouillis* is obtained. The operation is continued as long as there are any traces of alcohol. The working of the apparatus, Fig. 17, will be readily understood without description. The still with wine heater is figured in Fig. 18. It is com-

posed as follows : 1 is the still ; 2, 3, 4, 5, still head and
attachments ; 6, swan's neck ; 7, the worm in the condenser 8 ; 9 is the water funnel ; 10, strength regulator ; 11, overflow ; 12, mouth of the worm ; 14 is the
water bath ; 15, water gauge ; 16, wine heater ; 17,

FIG. 18.—BRANDY STILL WITH WINE HEATER.

cover of wine heater; 18, pipe for charging still. The brandy having been distilled, is sold to merchants who doctor it up to suit the taste of consumers and to give it the appearance of age. Not every kind of wood can be used for the casks, preference being given to the wood of Angoulême, which is more aromatic than the wood from places farther north.

Armagnac.—Under this name is comprised brandy distilled in Gers. It is sold at a strength of 52°, but like cognac it is distilled at a higher degree of strength. The manufacturers have very perfect apparatus, which permits of obtaining strong alcohol at the first distillation.

Brandy called Montpellier.—This is prepared in the outskirts of Béziers with choice white and red wines. It is sold of a strength equal to 52° to 66°. The apparatus used is very perfect.

Brandy of Marmande.—Under this name are included brandies made from the white wines in the neighborhood of Marmande. It has become scarce, has a peculiar taste, and is sold at a strength of 52°.

Marc Brandy.—Marc brandy is the product of the distillation of the marc of the grapes. The operation is usually performed with the aid of simple stills. However, improved apparatus is being introduced. Marc brandy has a high standard of about 60°. The principal centers of production are Bourgogne, Franche Comté, and Lorraine.

SECTION II.—FRUIT BRANDIES.

Kirsch or Kirschenwasser.—Kirsch or cherry brandy is prepared from the wild cherry; cultivated cherries give an equally good brandy, but much less perfumed than the wild cherry. The great centers of the manufacture in France are the department of Doubs, Haute-Saône, and Vosges; in Austria and Hungary, Transylvania, Dalmatia and the Black Forest. Dalmatia produces a kind of kirsch, known as maraschino, which differs from kirsch in the kind of cherry employed. The wild cherry (*Cerasus avium*) is indigenous in the forests of the Vosges and the Jura. It is cultivated chiefly on the eastern slopes, where the altitude varies from 500 to 800 meters. Young trees are also raised in nurseries. There are many varieties of wild cherries, but they are not all of equal value for the manufacture of kirsch. The cherries are gathered when they are perfectly ripe. This operation is performed by hand, and an able picker can gather about 50 kilogrammes a day. The harvest continues from eight to twelve days. The wild cherries are thrown into vats or into casks without heads, placed in a shed or other dry place.

The fermentation begins at the third or fourth day at latest, and continues for about a month. This fermentation ended, the wine is racked off and is not distilled until after fourteen days of rest. During this time the fermentation is finished.

The distillation is generally performed in an ordinary still (*i. e.*, with an alembic). The marc and the racked off juice are introduced in the neck of the alembic, which is then heated. This operation should be conducted with care, to prevent accident. The first portion of the distillate should be of a strength equal to 55° to 60°, and is placed in one vessel, and the second portion, which is intended to enrich the marc, by a second distillation in another.

Plum Brandy (Eau-de-vie de Prunes).—This liquor is prepared in France, Germany, in Hungary and Roumania from special varieties of plums that are called *couetache*. The other varieties of plums give a brandy as good but not as highly esteemed. The mode of preparation is the same as that of *kirsch* given above, but the product has more commercial importance than the cherry brandy.

Cider Brandy and Brandy from Pears.—This brandy is very highly esteemed in Normandy and Picardy, but is not very well known elsewhere.

SECTION III.—RUM AND TAFIA.

Under the name of rum a liquor was formerly understood which was obtained by distillation from sugar cane. This product has become very rare, and now the name *tafia* is applied to an alcohol prepared from the residues of a cane mill, the scum from clarification, molasses, etc. These materials are mixed with water or, better, with the products of a preceding distillation —a quantity sufficient to raise the must to 6° B. being used. This material is introduced into a vat or cask of small dimensions, and yeast is added. The fermentation is quickly done and the wine distilled in very simple stills (Fig. 19). The top is larger than the ordinary still, and is composed of three concentric rings, which augment the condensation of the vapors, and which also prevents a large portion of the odorous principles passing over with the alcohol.

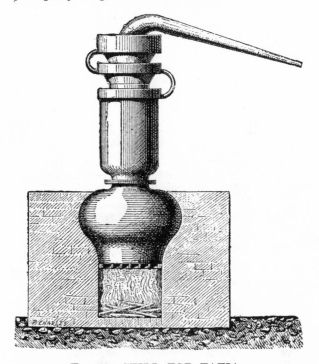

FIG. 19.—STILL FOR TAFIA.

M. Deroy (*fils ainé*) has constructed several forms of apparatus for distilling rum more perfectly than the simple still just described. This apparatus (Fig. 20) is composed of three pieces—the still, which has a large base; the head, with the "elephant's trunk;" and

the worm, which is placed in a tub or in a stone tank.
The heater is filled to about three-quarters of its capacity with the material to be distilled ; the joints of the
head are luted on.   The worm is cooled by cold water

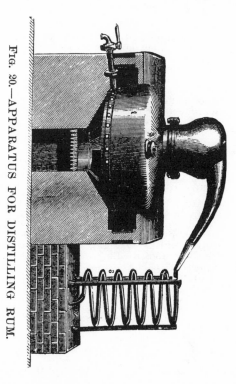

FIG. 20.—APPARATUS FOR DISTILLING RUM.

and the heating is commenced.   The distillation is
conducted slowly, so as to carry away the aqueous
vapors with the alcoholic.   The heating terminated,
the still is emptied by the cock, leaving only a little
liquid at the bottom.   M. Deroy has also devised two

other varieties of stills, one with a wine heater and
the other with a wine heater and an apparatus for
rectifying.

SECTION IV.—BRANDY FROM GRAIN.

(*Les Eau-de-vie de Grains.*)

In Belgium, Holland and England a brandy is prepared from grain which is known as gin or whisky.
The first is made of a mixture of malt and ungermin-
ated wheat; the second, the favorite liquor of the
Scotch and the Irish, is obtained from a mixture of
malt, rye and oats, or from corn. The distillation of
the must is conducted in the manner already described,
either with crude appliances or the most perfect apparatus that can be devised. The juniper or juniper
brandy is prepared by throwing into the must a
certain quantity of juniper berries. It appears that
it is not possible to stop the use of these berries in
preparing the liquor so dear to the inhabitants of the
North.

SECTION V.—THE NATURAL BRANDIES.

A list or table is given below of all the natural
liquors that are produced in various parts of the world,
with their origin and the principal place of consumption. [Our author's term *eau-de-vie* or brandy is very
comprehensive, whisky and gin, for instance, being
classed with the brandies.—Ed.]

Brandy, properly so called :
    Wine.—France.
Brandy from lees or potatoes :
    Glucose.—Northern Europe.
Brandy from beets :
    Juice, pulp or molasses from beets.—Northern
        Europe.
Brandy from rice :
    Saccharified rice.—Different countries.
Brandy from grains :
    Beers, saccharine grains.—All parts of the world.
Juniper :
    Beer, saccharine grains.—Belgium, Holland, Eng-
        land.
Schiedam :
    Saccharine grains, fermented, perfumed by juniper
        berries.—Holland.

Goldwasser :
> Brandy from grains, more or less perfumed.—Dantzig.

Whisky :
> Rye, oats, corn.—Scotland, Ireland, United States.

Kirschenwasser or kirsch :
> Fermented cherries.—France, Germany, Switzerland.

Maraschino :
> Cherries, fermented.—Zara.

Zwetschkenwasser :
> Plums (*couetache*), fermented.—France, Germany, Hungary.

Raki :
> Plums.—Hungary.

Rakia :
> Marc of grapes, perfumed.—Dalmatia.

Azaka, Arza, Arka, or Ariki :
> Mare's milk, fermented.—Tartary.

Tafia :
> From molasses.—Antilles.

Rack or Arrack :
> Must of cane sugar.—Hindostan.

Rum :
> Must of cane sugar, molasses.—Antilles.

Aqua-ardiente or Pulque Fuerte :
> Juice of the Agave.—Mexico and South America.

M. De Brevans names twenty-five additional ones, but they are of little importance, being mostly Asiatic drinks of the Chinese.

SECTION VI.—ARTIFICIAL BRANDIES.

The production of true brandy having decreased and the demand increased is clear proof that a large part of the modern brandies are simply a mixture of alcohol with various substances calculated to give the taste of true brandy. Various receipts are given, but the base of the adulterated article is a mixture of cachou (cashoo, a kind of resin), vanilla, green walnut shells, balsam of tolu, orris, essence of bitter almonds, rum and old kirsch, sirup of grapes, sassafras, broom plant, maidenhair, licorice, etc. In order to obtain artificially the effect of age, it is necessary to make an infusion of oak shavings. This is used in connection with molasses or caramel for coloring matters.

PART II.—ARTIFICIAL LIQUORS.

CHAPTER I.

THE PLANT OF THE DISTILLER.

THE laboratory of the *liquoriste* or distiller should be of sufficient size to enable him to carry on his work with facility. The walls should be well built and of sufficient height to prevent the flames from burning the ceiling in case of fire. The laboratory should be well ventilated, lighted from above and paved with brick, stone or gravel. An abundant supply of water should be at hand. The chimney must be large and well constructed and should terminate in a hood, under this are placed the stills (Fig. 21, A, B). The chemist should have a small private laboratory (13) where he can make his experiments. The plant in this small laboratory is very simple: A furnace surmounted by a hood, some gas burners, an alembic, a case of reagents, a good balance, a case for fine instruments, and a work table. In the plan illustrated herewith the store rooms ought to be as far away as possible, on the same floor as the laboratory. They should not be damp and the temperature should be maintained between 12 and 15° (C.) The floor is generally graveled or paved with asphalt.

The cellars must be well ventilated, have a northern exposure and a depth of 5 or 6 meters.

Figs. 22 and 23 represent a large distillery at Saint Denis, for the manufacture of liquors. In Fig. 22 a battery of stills of medium size are shown, the worms having a condensing tank in common. Fig. 23 is a view in another part of the distillery in which the large basins are set up, as well as the stills and the receivers for the raw materials. As the operation of a number of stills has been described, it will not be necessary to describe them again. The operations of the distiller require a large assortment of basins of copper, both tinned and untinned, steam-heated basins and basins

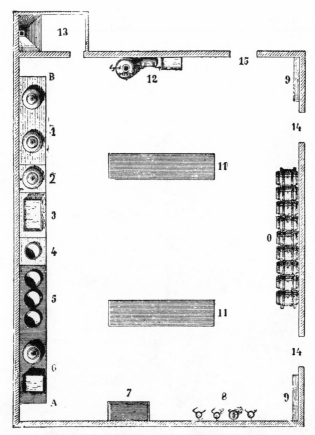

Fig. 21.—PLAN OF A DISTILLERY.

1. Steam stills. 2. Stills for open fires. 3. Common condenser. 4. Heating basin (open fire). 5. Basins heated with a water bath. 6. Independent still. 7. Digester for making preserves. 8. Filters and digesters. 9. Closets. 10. Casks. 11. Work tables. 12. Steam generator. 13. Private laboratory.

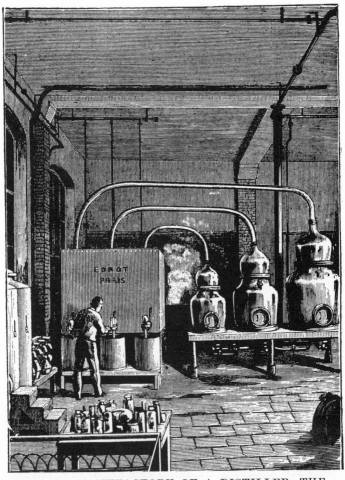

FIG. 22.—MANUFACTORY OF A DISTILLER—THE
STILLS—INSTALLATION BY EGROT.

FIG. 23.—MANUFACTORY OF A DISTILLER.

FIG. 24.—COPPER BASIN.

FIG. 25.—OSCILLATING BASIN FOR STEAM.

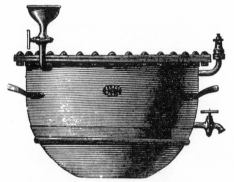

FIG. 26.—COPPER BASIN WITH DOUBLE
BOTTOM, VALVES, PIPES, ETC.

FIG. 27.—FIXED BASIN FOR STEAM.

heated by an open fire (Figs. 24, 25, 26, 27), skimmers, spatulas, an assortment of alcoholometers and hydrometers, mortars, balances, etc.

The filtration of raw materials and the finished pro-

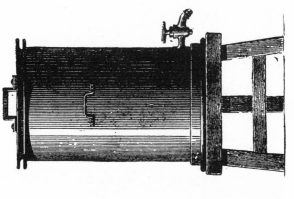

FIG. 30.

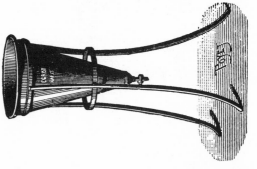

FIG. 28.—FILTER HOLDER.

ducts requires the use of bone black filters. Fig. 28 represents one of the large tinned funnels terminated in a cock. The distiller must have at his disposal a series of siphons of different sizes in glass or metal. Fig. 29 represents a siphon of large size, and it is very convenient for transferring alcohol. The reservoirs or

holders of raw materials and finished products are
made of tinned copper (Fig. 30).   A scale placed on the
outside and a gauge glass determine the amount of

FIG. 29.—BELLOWS AND COMPRESSED AIR SYSTEM FOR MOVING LIQUIDS.

the liquid inside. A perfect holder and distributor is
illustrated in the SCIENTIFIC AMERICAN SUPPLE-
MENT, No. 516.

CHAPTER II.

Raw Materials.

SECTION I.—ALCOHOL.

In the useful arts the name spirits is given to alcohols which mark 70° on the alcoholometer of Gay-Lussac, the only legal standard recognized in France since the law of July 8, 1881, rendered effective by the decree of December 27, 1884. In commercial language, the different spirits are known under the names $\frac{3}{5}$, $\frac{3}{6}$, $\frac{3}{7}$, $\frac{3}{8}$, which are derived from an old method of estimating the strength of alcohol relating to brandy, called *preuve de Hollande*, marking 19° Cartier, which included about 50 per cent. of the volume of absolute alcohol. As we have already seen, spirits are produced from the distillation of wine, beets, molasses, grain, and potatoes. The distiller, or rather *liquoriste*, requires to make at least, if not absolutely, neutral spirits of good taste, because it is evident that if the spirits (alcohol) used have a pronounced taste, it will materially affect the product.

The principal kinds of alcohol used in France are named as follows: $\frac{3}{6}$ commercial = 85° G.-L.

The $\frac{3}{6}$ Languedoc.—Alcohol distilled from wine, strength 86°, very scarce at the present day. Used principally in making cognacs.

The $\frac{3}{6}$ Neutral, or Extra Fine.—Alcohol obtained by the rectification of alcohol, particularly from rice. It is of a strength equal to 90° to 95°.

The $\frac{3}{6}$ Fine of the North.—Alcohol from beets, rectified. It nearly always has a taste of the beet root. The spirits obtained by treating molasses are preferable. This alcohol is generally sold at 90°.

SECTION II.—ESSENCES.

Essences, or essential oils, have an oily look, generally very volatile, and are produced from a large number of substances in the vegetable kingdom, producing the odor of the plant. Their chemical composition is very complex. All odorous materials are generally very volatile, but at different temperatures. Their vapor tension is considerable, which explains the diffusion of the odor of flowers, as well as aromatic plants, to great distances. The essences are very volatile, as already stated, and are in the liquid form at ordinary temperatures, except in rare cases. The greater part are uncolored, but some are colored yellow, brown, green, and even blue, all are soluble in alcohol, ether, chloroform, and light hydrocarbons; but, to speak properly, they

FIG. 31.—SCREW PRESS FOR OILS.

are not dissolved in water, they are diffused only—that is to say, distilled waters owe their perfume only to minute drops of the essence, which are held in suspension, but it is not a perfectly homogeneous mixture, as the mixture of sugar and water.

Light has a certain action on essence. The air, by its oxygen, produces a great change, more or less rapid.

producing a difference in the odor and a gradual resin-ification. The essences have variable specific gravi-ties, some being lighter and some heavier than water. These points are very valuable when testing for adul-terating materials.

Extraction of Essences.—The manufacture of es-sences is an industry of warm countries, and is exten-sively carried on at Grasse, Nice, and Cannes. Cer-tain plants, such as the mint, are largely cultivated

FIG. 32.—ZESTEUSE OF LESOULT.

in the regions of the north. The industry of perfume making is, as is well known, of great antiquity, and the process has remained almost unchanged until the present day. The processes of extraction are expres-sion, distillation, maceration, and enfleurage.

Expression is a simple process, but it is rarely used, as it can only be profitably employed when the plant is rich in volatile oils. The skins of oranges and ci-trons are examples. The parts rich in essences are placed under the press, and the oils are extracted mechanically (Fig. 31). The mixture collects a good deal of water, but by repose, the essences separate and are removed by decantation (Fig. 33). In expression a piece of apparatus for removing the rind of fruit (Fig. 32) is sometimes used. It is called in French a *zesteuse*. The pedals actuate two graters, which remove the skin in a short space of time.

Distillation is of ancient origin, and the apparatus used in the manufacture of essential oils is often very crude, and only recently has the naked fire given place to steam as a source of heat. The products of distillation are usually received in flasks (Fig. 33), called Flor-

FIG. 33.—FLORENTINE RECEIVER—
DOUBLE EFFECT.

entine receivers, which permit of the separation of the essential oil from the water. The watery portion contains a certain proportion of essence which cannot be removed; but this water can itself be used for a perfume. It is in this manner that rose water, orange flower water and others *can* be prepared. The delicate plants are treated as follows : The interior of the still is divided by a diaphragm pierced with holes, on which the plants are placed, this being submitted only to the action of the vapor which rises from below. The products are received as before. Distillation cannot be used for many plants, as the essential oil would be decomposed by a temperature of at least 100° C.

Maceration is applied to those substances which cannot stand a high temperature without being decomposed. This operation is performed by plunging the plants or flowers in a bath of old or fine fat, treated gently on a water bath. The fatty materials receive the essence and a perfumed oil or pomade is the result, and the essence can be extracted from this by means of alcohol. Paraffine is largely used at the present day. Rectangular frames with glass bottoms are used, the size being about 0·97 m. long by 0·64 m. wide. The fat is laid on the glass to a thickness of 0·0067 m., the flowers are thrown on this and they are allowed to remain from 12 to 72 hours, the flowers being changed as often as necessary. If the oil is used, the plates of glass are replaced by coarse linen saturated with oil. When the operation of absorbing the odor of the flowers by the oil is finished, the oil is obtained by pressure. To shorten this long operation M. Piver has invented the following apparatus. A square closet 2 × 3 meters in size is divided longitudinally into two parts, communicating with each other. Wire cloth screens receive the fat. Between each screen a thin sheet of glass or tinned copper is secured at one side only. This receives the flowers. The fat which is placed on the wire gauze is converted into thin, vermicelli-like threads. The flowers are placed upon the tinned copper plates and the closet is closed. Two pairs of bellows, one on each half, keep up a current of air. By this method the fat absorbs the perfume from the air with great rapidity, thereby obviating the danger of the fat becoming rancid. For several years past, the two methods of procedure just given have been displaced by a process which permits of relieving the plants of their odors in a very short time. The solvents are chloroform, sulphide of carbon, petroleum ethers, methyl chloride, etc. This invention is due to M. Millon and has since been perfected by MM. Piver and Naudin. The process comprises three operations : 1. The dissolving process ; 2, distillation at a low temperature ; 3, the evaporation of the last traces of the solvent. Fig. 34 represents the apparatus. The odorous parts of plants or flowers are introduced into a digester, A, being inclosed in a wire basket, E. A vacuum is obtained by means of a pump, D′, and by means of this vacuum a known quantity of the solvent is brought up from R, by the tube nn'. After having

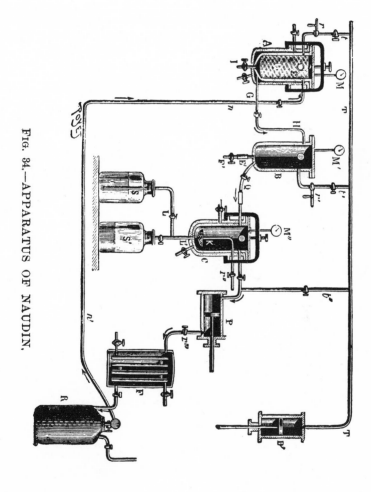

FIG. 34.—APPARATUS OF NAUDIN.

placed the materials in contact with the solvent for a period not exceeding a quarter of an hour, the liquid is passed from A into B, by means of a vacuum. The water coming from the flowers is decanted by means of I. The tube, E', permits an easy separation of the various liquids. Communication is established between B and C, and also with the refrigerator or condenser, F. In the course of the distillation the temperature of evaporation is at that of the atmosphere, which is accomplished by a current of water. All the solvents are rapidly evaporated in C, and condensed in F, leaving the perfume in C. The solvent which was condensed is run into the receptacle, R. If the distillation has been made at a temperature sufficiently low, the liquid solvent will not retain any appreciable trace of the odor, and can be used again for different perfumes. The perfume mixed with the waxy substances of flowers and leaves must be dissolved by the preceding method. The wax is dissolved by ether. A quantity of alcohol contained in S is brought up by a vacuum. After a digestion of two hours, the liquid is thrown into the vessel, S, which precipitates the wax, while the perfume remains dissolved in the alcohol. The product is then filtered. In this process the liquid never comes into contact with the air.

Purification of Essences.—The raw essence cannot be employed without purification. Two cases come before the distiller, one in which the raw essences are dealt with and the other when they have become rancid. The first case is remedied in three ways :

1. The separation of essence by alcoholic vapors.

2. Congelation, which permits of separation by means of the different degrees of solidification.

3. Oxidation of essences by the use of the proper chemicals, as water, oxygen, permanganate of potassium, etc.

M. Duplais has indicated the proper manner of restoring essential oils when they have become rancid. The volatile rancid oil is placed in a still along with a large quantity of the recent plant and a sufficient quantity of water. The still is then started. The volatile oil is saturated anew with the perfume, and passes over with the fresh volatile oil from the plants. When a volatile oil is not entirely changed, but has commenced to lose color and limpidity, it is sufficient, in order to restore it, to pour it into a small glass retort

placed in a sand bath on a furnace. The receiver is
attached and distillation is proceeded with at a moderate heat, about equal to that of boiling water. The
volatile oil which passes over is limpid and almost
without color. The distillation is stopped when the
drops begin to be colored. What remains in the retort is
thick and has the appearance of a resin.

TABLE OF THE PRINCIPAL ESSENCES.

The following gives a synoptic view of the principal
essences, according to M. Basset. The French names
are also given, and the order of M. De Brevans is
retained.

Essences Lighter than Water.

Absinthe (Large). *Grande Absinthe.*
> The entire plant, used fresh, dark green, odor pro-
> nounced, grows darker with age.

Absinthe (Small). *Petite Absinthe.*
> Entire plant, used fresh, lighter green, odor weaker
> than the *Grande Absinthe.*

Anise. *Aneth.*
> Dry seeds, no color, pronounced odor of anise.

Anise (Green). *Anis vert.*
> Dry seeds, no color, odor of the seed, crystallizes
> at +12° C., easily decomposed.

Angelica. *Angélique.*
> Fresh plant, no color, odor of the plant, darkens
> with age.

Elecampane. *Aunée.*
> Dry roots, yellow, odor of camphor, white when
> old.

Anise (Chinese). *Badiane.*
> Dry seed, colorless; odor resembles that of anise
> a little; crystallizes at +15° C., turns yellow with
> age.

Basilic.
> Entire plant, golden yellow, odor of the plant,
> darkens with age.

Bergamot. *Bergamote.*
> Fresh skins, by distillation, colorless, odor of the
> fruit.

Birch. *Bouleau.*
> Bark, colorless, very agreeable odor, resinifies
> when old.

Calamint. *Calament.*
> Flower of the fresh plant, weak odor of mint.

Calamus.
    Fresh roots, yellow, weak odor of camphor.
Camomile.
    Fresh flowers, blue, little odor.
Cardamom (Large). *Grand Cardamome.*
    Dry seed, light yellow, odor of musk.
Cardamom (Small). *Petit Cardamome.*
    Dry seeds, light yellow, pronounced odor of musk.
Caraway. *Carvi.*
    Dry seeds, light yellow, odor of the seed.
Cascarilla.
    Dry bark, light yellow, odor of musk, bitter taste.
Cedrat. (Kind of Lemon.)
    Fresh skins, by distillation, almost colorless, odor
      of the fruit.
Lemon. *Citron.*
    Fresh skins, by distillation, almost colorless, odor
      of the fruit, becomes thick and resinifies with
      age.
Coriander. *Coriandre.*
    Dry seed, yellowish, odor of the seed.
Cumin.
    Dry seeds, yellowish, odor of the seed, sour, acid
      taste.
Curaçao.
    Dried skin of Seville oranges, yellowish, odor of
      the fruit, taste bitter, thickens with age.
Fennel. *Fenouil.*
    Dry seeds, clear yellow, odor of the seeds, crystal-
      lizes at $+6°$ C.
Juniper. *Genievre.*
    Fresh berries, colorless, trace of the odor of va-
      nilla.
Ginger. *Gingembre.*
    Dried root, yellowish green, odor of the root, burn-
      ing taste.
Heliotrope.
    Fresh flowers, weak odor of vanilla.
Hyssop.
    Tops of flowers, yellowish, agreeable odor.
Lavender.
    Tops of the fresh flowers, yellowish green, strong
      odor of the plant, darkens with age.
Marjoram. *Marjolaine.*
    Fresh plants in flower, clear yellow, agreeable odor
      of camphor.

Melissa (Balm Mint). *Mélisse* or *Citronella.*
Flowering plant, almost colorless, odor of lemon,
acrid taste.

Peppermint. *Menthe Poivrée.*
Tops of the flowering plants, colorless, odor of the
plant, crystallizes between $+21°$ and $+22°$ C.,
turns yellow with age, taste fresh and sharp.

Nutmeg. *Muscade.*
Dried fruit, yellow; the essence has a slight odor
of musk.

Orange Tree. *Oranges.*
Fresh flowers, yellow, odor of the flower, color
changes to brownish red with time.

Oranges.
Fresh fruit, skins, by distillation or expression,
light yellow, odor of the skin.

Rosewood. *Bois de Rhodes.*
Dry wood, yellow, odor of the rose, bitter taste,
reddens and resinifies with age.

Rosemary. *Romarin.*
Fresh flowering plant, greenish yellow, odor of the
plant, with a trace of camphor, burning taste.

Rose.
Fresh petals, almost colorless, agreeable odor of
the rose, crystallizes below $+10°$ C.

Sage. *Sauge.*
Fresh plant, yellow to green, odor of camphor and
of the plant, turns dark with age.

Tansy. *Tanaisie.*
Fresh flowering plant, yellowish green, odor and
taste of anise and fennel.

Thyme. *Serpolet.*
Fresh flowering plant, greenish yellow, odor of the
plant, turns brown with age.

Essences Heavier than Water.

Bitter Almond. *Amandes Amères.*
Pressed oil cakes, pale yellow, odor of the kernel,
changes with time, and oxidizes, poisonous.

Cinnamon (Ceylon). *Cannelle de Ceylan.*
Dried bark, yellow, odor of cinnamon.

Cinnamon (Chinese). *Cannelle de Chine.*
Dried bark, yellow, odor of cinnamon, less agreeable than the preceding.

Celery. *Celeri.*
Dried seeds, reddish brown, strong, sharp odor of
the plant.

Clove. *Girofle.*
> Dry fruit, yellow, pronounced odor of cloves, sharp taste.

Mace. *Macis.*
> Golden yellow, odor of thyme, pepperish taste.

Nutmeg. *Muscade.*
> Odor of nutmeg very pronounced when the essence is separated from the lighter portion.

Parsley. *Persil.*
> Dry seeds, yellow to green, odor of the plant, bitter taste.

Saffron. *Safran.*
> Yellow, odor of the plant, decomposes and resinifies with time.

Sassafras.
> Dried root, reddish yellow, odor of the root, turns red with age.

Zedoary (Wild Ginger). *Zédoaire.*
> Dried roots, pale yellow, odor of camphor, darkens in color with age.

As the result of many experiments, the following has been found to be product of essence for each 10 kilogrammes of materials used :

	Grammes.		Grammes.
Absinthe, large..............	12	to	12·5
Absinthe, small........	4·5	"	5
Almonds, bitter......	18	"	60
Angelica....................	28	"	—
Anise, green..................	118	"	200
Anise, Chinese	112	"	430
Camomile	8·4	"	40
Caraway...............	350	"	400
Cardamom, small..........	200	"	—
Cascarilla	62·5	"	87
Cinnamon, Ceylon....	75	"	170
Cinnamon, China............	22	"	75
Coriander...	13	"	14
Fennel	21	"	23
Juniper...............	48	"	85
Laurel......................	32	"	80
Mace....	12	"	60
Nutmeg, butter..	350	"	360
Orange.......................	5	"	30
Peppermint.......	70	"	—
Rose...............	0·4	"	1·6
Sassafras....	6·4	"	50
Tansy...............	30	"	—

SECTION III.—PERFUMED SPIRITS.

This name is given to alcohol which is charged with odorous principles. They are known in French as *alcoolats*. Alcoholates in pharmacy are simple perfumed spirits. Essence is a better term than perfumed spirit,

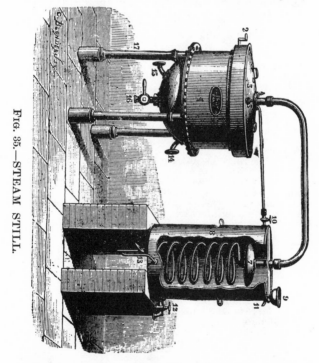

FIG. 35.—STEAM STILL.

and essence will be used throughout this section instead of spirit (French *esprit*).

Essences are of two kinds, simple and compound.

Simple Essences.—The apparatus for making aromatic essences is generally heated by a water bath or by steam (Fig. 35). This last method is admirably adapted for large works.   To prepare simple essences, the substances, which have been previously cut, contused, or pulverized, as the case may be, are placed in the still.   The necessary alcohol is then introduced, and after twenty-four hours of maceration, a certain quantity of water is added, and the distillation is started, and is only stopped when all the alcohol has passed over.   The product should have an equal bulk as the alcohol which was put in, plus the amount of water added.

In general, the preparation of essences is as follows-- the proportion of materials being about as follows :

Raw material ....   1 k.
Alcohol, at 85' ... .   5 l.

After maceration, 2 l. 500 c. c. of water are put in and distilled, so as to obtain 5 l. of essence.   This is mixed with 2 l. 500 c. c. and rectified so as to allow a product of 4 l.

The backings, or phlegm, which form the last products of distillation and rectification, are placed aside for another operation.   The abbreviations for the metric system adopted are as follows :

Grm. = gramme or grammes ; k. = kilogrammes ; c. c. = cubic centimeters ; l. = liters.   For tables for converting metric into United States standard measures, see the Appendix.   Both the English and French names will be given where they differ.

Essence of Absinthe (large or small).
Esprit de Grande Absinthe.

Leaves and dry tops of the
   large or small absinthe.......   2 k. 500 grm.
Alcohol (85°).................. ....   10 l. 500 c. c.
Water.... ....   5 l.
           Product : 10 l.

Essence of Aloes.
Esprit d'Aloes.

Socotrine aloes ....   600 grm.
Alcohol (85°). ....   10 l. 500 c. c.
Water... ....   5 l.
           Product : 10 l.

Essence Bitter Almonds.
Esprit d'Amandes Ameres.

Bitter almonds..............	2 k. 500 grm.
Alcohol (85°)...........	10 l. 500 c. c.
Water.....	5 l.

Product : 10 l.

Essence of Amber Seed.
Esprit d'Ambrette.

Grain amber seed.......	1 k. 250 grm.
Alcohol (85°)..................	10 l. 500 c. c.
Water.........	5 l.

Product : 10 l.

Anise, star anise, angelica, and others are prepared as directed above.

Essence of Benzoin.
Esprit de Benjoin.

Benzoin in tears...............	600 grm.
Alcohol (85°)....	10 l. 500 c. c.
Water.................. .. .	5 l.

Product : 10 l.

Essence of Bergamot.
Esprit d'Bergamote.

Bergamot......................	4 k. 500 grm.
Alcohol (85°)............	10 l. 500 c. c.
Water.........	5 l.

Product : 10 l.

Essence of Catechu.
Esprit de Cachou.

Catechu, Japanese, pulverized.	600 grm.
Alcohol (85°)............	10 l. 500 c. c.
Water....	5 l.

Product : 10 l.

Essence of Cinnamon (Ceylon).
Esprit de Cannelle de Ceylon.

Pulverized cinnamon..........	300 grm.
Alcohol (85°).................	10 l. 500 c. c.
Water....	5 l.

Macerate for 24 hours, distill over an open fire, rectify the product with 5 l. of water over the open fire.

Essence of Cinnamon (Chinese).
Esprit de Cannelle de Chine.

Cinnamon, pulverized .... 300 grm.
Alcohol (85°).................... 10 l. 500 c. c.
Water. .... 5 l.

Prepare same as the Ceylon cinnamon.

Essence of Cardamom (large).
Esprit de Grand Cardamone.

Seeds of large cardamon (*Amo-
miun cardamomum*)......... 600 grm.
Alcohol (85°).................... 10 l. 500 c. c.
Water.................. ... 5 l.
Product : 10 l.

Essence of Cardamon (small).
Esprit de Petit Cardamone.

Preparation same as above.

Essence of Caraway.
Esprit de Carvi.

Caraway seeds. .... 1 k. 250 grm.
Alcohol (85°).................... 10 l. 500 c. c.
Water.. .... 5 l.
Product : 10 l.

Essence of Cascarilla.

Prepared in the same way as the above.

Essence of Cedrat.
Esprit de Cédrats.

Fresh rinds or skins of......... 60 cedrats.
Alcohol (85°)............. .... 12 l.

Macerate for 24 hours, add 5 l. of water, and distill so
as to make 11 l.; rectify with 5 l. of water.
Product : 10 l.

Essence of Celery.
Esprit de Céleri.

Celery seed..... .. .. 1 k. 250 grm.
Alcohol (85°).... . ... 10 l. 500 c. c.
Product : 10 l.

Essence of Lemon.
Esprit de Citron.

Fresh skins of ... ...   80 lemons
Alcohol (85°) ....   12 l.

Proceed in the same manner as for essence of cedrat.
Product : 10 l.

Concentrated Essence of Lemon.
Esprit de Citron Concentré.

Fresh skins of ....   160 lemons
Alcohol (85°) ... ...   12 l.

Same method as above.

Essence of Coriander.

Coriander seeds ....   2 k. 500 grm.
Alcohol (85°) ....   10 l. 50 c. c.
Water...........................   5 l.
Product : 10 l.

Essence of Cumin Seeds.
Esprit de Cumin.

Cumin seeds...................   1 k. 250 grm.
Alcohol (85°) ....   10 l. 500 c. c.
Water...........................   5 l.
Product : 10 l.

Essence of Curaçao.

Rinds of Curaçao oranges......   2 k.
Alcohol (85°).. ....   12 l.
Water.....   ....   5 l.

Macerate for 36 hours.
Product : 10 l.

Essence of Candy Carrot.
Esprit de Daucus.

Seeds of candy carrot, from
  Crete. .. ..   1 k. 250 grm.
Alcohol (85°)..................   10 l. 500 c. c.
Water...........................   5 l.
Product : 10 l.

Essence of Fennel.
Esprit de Fenouil.

This is prepared in the same manner as essence of cinnamon.

Essence of Genepi.
Esprit de Génépi.

Leaves and tops of Alpine genepi..............	1 k. 250 grm.
Alcohol (85°).............	10 l. 500 c. c.
Water........	5 l.

Product : 10 l.

Essence of Ginger, Essence of Juniper.
Esprit de Gingembre, Esprit de Genièvre.

Same method of preparation as essence of genepi.

Essence of Cloves.
Esprit de Girofle.

Bruised cloves	60 grm.
Alcohol (85°)	10 l. 500 c. c.
Water.............	5 l.

Proceed the same as for cinnamon.

Product : 10 l.

Essence of Hyssop.
Esprit d'Hysope.

Dried flowering tops of hyssop..	2 k. 500 grm.
Alcohol (85°)...............	10 l. 500 c. c.
Water...................... ...	5 l.

Product : 10 l.

Essence of Lavender.
Esprit de Lavande.

Dried flowering lavender tops..	1 k. 250 grm.
Alcohol (85°)	10 l. 500 c. c.
Water...........	5 l.

Product : 10 l.

Essence of Mace.
Esprit de Macis.

Crushed mace..................	600 grm.
Alcohol (85°).............	10 l. 500 c. c.
Water.........	5 l.

Product : 10 l.

Essence of Balm.
Esprit de Mélisse.

Picked and dried balm.........	2 k. 500 grm.
Alcohol (85°)....................	10 l. 500 c. c.
Water.	5 l.

Product : 10 l.

Essence of Mint.
Esprit de Menthe.

Prepared in the same manner as the above, with the flowering tops of dried peppermint.

Essence of Mocha or Essence of Coffee.
Esprit de Moka.

Martinique and Mocha coffee equal parts mixed	1 k. 250 grm.
Alcohol (85°)...............	10 l. 500 c. c.
Water...............	5 l.

Brown the coffee until it is of a fine yellow; then grind coarse and macerate for 24 hours. Distill so as to draw off 12 l., then rectify.

Product : 10 l.

Essence of Myrrh.
Esprit de Myrrhe.

Pulverized myrrh	600 grm.
Alcohol (85°)....	10 l. 500 c. c.
Water....	5 l.

Product : 10 l.

Essence of Apricot Seeds.
Esprit de Noyaux d'Abricots.

Kernels of seeds of apricots crushed	2 k. 500 grm.
Alcohol (85°).............	10 l. 500 c. c.
Water.........	5 l.

Product : 10 l.

Essence of Nutmegs.
Esprit de Muscade.

Nutmegs, crushed	600 grm.
Alcohol (85°)	10 l. 500 c. c.
Water.	5 l.

Same mode of preparation as essence of cinnamon.

Product : 10 l.

Essence of Pinks.
Esprit d' Oeillets.

Petals of pinks, cleansed.......	2 k.	500 grm.
Alcohol (85°).................	10 l.	500 c. c.
Water....................... ...	5 l.	

Product : 10 l.

Essence of Orange Flowers.
Esprit d' Oranger.

Orange flowers, cleansed.......	2 k.	500 grm.
Alcohol (85°)...................	10 l.	500 c. c.
Water.	5 l.	

Product : 10 l.

Essence of Orange.
Esprit d' Oranger.

Fresh peel of 100 oranges.

Alcohol (85°)...	12 l.
Water	5 l.

Product : 10 l.

Same operation as in making essence of lemons.

Essence of Orange (concentrated).

Fresh peel of 200 oranges.
Operation same as above.

Essence of Rosewood.
Esprit de Bois de Rhodes.

Shavings of rosewood	600 grm.	
Alcohol (85°)....................	10 l.	500 c. c.
Water........................	5 l.	

Product : 10 l.

Essence of Roses.
Esprit de Roses.

Fresh rose leaves..............	5 k.	
Alcohol (85°)................	10 l.	500 c. c.
Water	5 l.	

Product : 10 l.

Essence of Saffron.
Esprit de Safran.

Saffron (*du Gatinais*) 1st quality	300 grm.	
Alcohol (85°)....................	10 l. 500 c. c.	

Product : 10 l.

Essence of Sandal Wood.
Esprit de Santal.

Sandal wood broken up (lemon colored).	600 grm.
Alcohol (85°)	10 l. 500 c. c.
Water	5 l.

Product : 10 l.

Essence of Sassafras.

Sassafras root cut fine, 600 grm. Same method of procedure as for sandal wood.

Essence of Tea.
Esprit de Thé.

Tea (Pekao)	100 grm.
" (Hyson)	100 grm.
" (Imperial)	200 grm.
Alcohol (85°)	10 l. 500 c. c.
Water	5 l.

Make an infusion in boiling water and let it stand in a closed vessel for two hours ; add the alcohol, distill and rectify.

Product : 10 l.

Essence of Tolu.
Esprit de Tolu.

Balsam of tolu	600 grm.
Alcohol (85°)	10 l. 50 c. c.
Water	5 l.

Compound Essences.

Compound essences are numerous. They are prepared in the same manner as simple essences.

Compound Essence of Absinthe.
Esprit d'Absinthe Composé.

Absinthe, cleaned	1000 grm.
Juniper, crushed	125 grm.
Cinnamon (Ceylon)	30 grm.
Angelica root.	8 grm.
Alcohol (85°)	5 l.

Macerate for twelve days and distill. Draw off 3 l. 50 c. c. of the product. Redistill slowly to obtain 3 l. of product.

Compound Essence of Anisette (Ordinary).
Esprit d'Anisette Ordinaire.

Green anise...	600 grm.
Chinese (star) anise............	600 grm.
Fennel	200 grm.
Coriander	200 grm.
Alcohol (85°)...................	10 l. 500 c. c.

Mix the dry bruised materials, macerate for 36 hours. Put on 5 l. of water and distill so as to obtain 10 l. 500 c. c. To this product add 5 l. of water and rectify to obtain 10 l.

Essence of Bordeaux Anisette.
Esprit d'Anisette de Bordeaux.

Green anise.	400 grm.
Chinese anise.................	100 grm.
Fennel	100 grm.
Coriander	100 grm.
Sassafras....................	100 grm.
Amber seed (*ambrette*)..........	25 grm.
Tea (imperial)......	grm.
Alcohol (85°)..................	10 l. 500 c. c.

Essence or Elixir of Garus.
Esprit de Gorus (Codex).

Alcohol (80°)...	6 l.
Socotrine aloes................	5 grm.
Saffron...........	5 grm.
Myrrh....	2 grm.
Cinnamon.........	20 grm.
Cloves.......................	5 grm.
Nutmegs......	18 grm.

Mix the bruised materials and macerate for four days in alcohol, filter, put in 1 l. of water and distill so as to draw off the spirituous portion.

Compound Essence of Juniper.
Esprit de Genièvre Composé.

Juniper....	500 grm.
Caraway	60 grm.
Fennel....	60 grm.
Alcohol (15°)..................	4 l. 500 c. c.

Bruise the materials, macerate for 24 hours in alcohol, add 1 l. of water and distill to obtain 4 l. 500 c. c. Rectify to obtain 4 l.

SECTION IV.—ALCOHOLIC TINCTURES.

Under the name of tinctures are included substances which are obtained by the maceration of aromatic plants in alcohol. They are of two kinds—true alcoholic tinctures, prepared from the dry materi-

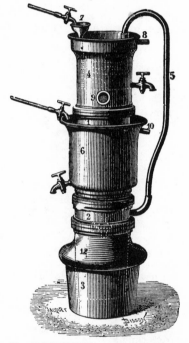

FIG. 36.—DIGESTOR OR EXTRACTOR.

als, and spirits (Fr. *alcoolatures*), prepared from fresh materials.

Tinctures are divided into two classes, simple and compound.

Maceration is accomplished by leaving the materials

for a greater or less time in contact with the solvent by means of digestors or extractors (Fig. 36). The plants are placed in the cylinder of digestion, a quantity of alcohol is introduced and the apparatus is heated. The alcohol distilled is condensed in the neck of the still and is returned and the process is repeated continuously. By this operation the alcohol is constantly brought into contact with the materials until it has dissolved as much as possible of the principles of the plant.

Tincture of Absinthe.
Teinture d'Absinthe.

Dry leaves and tops of absinthe
    (small)............................ 260 grm.
Alcohol (85°)......................... 1 l.

Macerate for 14 days. Agitate daily and filter.

Tincture of Aloes.
Teinture d'Aloès.

Cape aloes............................ 200 grm.
Alcohol (60)........................ 1 l.

Macerate for 8 hours and filter.

Tincture Bitter Almonds.
Teinture d'Amandes Amères.

Shells of bitter almonds.......... . 500 grm.
Alcohol (85°)........ .... 1 l.

Pile the shells up and macerate for a month at least in alcohol, agitating daily, and filter.

Tincture of Ambergris.
Teinture d'Ambre.

Gray ambergris....................... 16 grm.
Alcohol (85°)........... .... 1 l.

Macerate for 14 days with gentle heat (25 to 30° C.) and agitate from time to time.

Tincture of Angelica.
Teinture d'Angélique.

Roots of angelica, crushed.............. 200 grm.
Alcohol (85°) .... 50 c. c.

Macerate at 25° C. or thereabout and decant the product. Macerate again for five days and repeat with a half liter of 85 per cent. alcohol. Extract tincture with the aid of pressure, unite the two parts and filter.

Tincture of Anise.
Teinture d'Anis.

Green anise crushed .... 250 grm.
Alcohol (85°) .... 1 l.
Macerate for 10 days and filter.

Tincture of Benzoin.
Teinture de Benjoin.

Benzoin in tears, pulverized .... 125 grm.
Alcohol (85°) .... 1 l.
Same method of preparation as that used in making tincture of ambergris.
Tinctures of tolu, storax and cachou are prepared in the same manner.

Tincture of Cinnamon.
Teinture de Cannelle.

Crushed cinnamon .. .. 100 grm.
Alcohol (85°) .... 1 l.
Macerate the cinnamon in the alcohol for eight days at a temperature of 25 to 30°.
In the same manner are prepared the tincture of cardamom, cascarilla, coriander, mace, musk, etc.

Tincture of Curaçao.
Teinture de Curaçao.

Peel of curaçao (of Holland) .... 500 grm.
Alcohol (85°) .... 1 l.
Macerate, stir daily and filter.

Tincture of Galangal.
Teinture de Galanga.

Bruised roots of galangal ... . 750 grm.
Alcohol (50°) .... 1 l.
Macerate after 14 days, filter.

Tincture of Hyssop.
Teinture d'Hysope.

Dried flowering tops of hyssop .... 250 grm.
Alcohol (85°) .... 1 l.
Macerate in the alcohol for 14 days, shaking frequently, then filter.

Tincture of Orris.
Teinture d'Iris.

Florentine orris pulverized..	125 grm.
Alcohol (85°).........	1 l.

Macerate for 14 days, then filter.

Tincture of Laurel.
Teinture de Laurier.

Leaves of laurel, dry and cut fine.....	125 grm.
Alcohol (50°).....	1 l.

Macerate for 14 days, filter.

Tincture of Balm.
Teinture de Mélisse.

Dried leaves of the yellow balm......	250 grm.
Alcohol (85°).........	1 l.

Macerate for 10 days and agitate, daily filter.

Tincture of Musk.
Teinture de Musc.

Tonkin musk	8 grm.
Alcohol (85°)	1 l.

Macerate 10 days, shaking frequently, filter.

Tincture of Vanilla.
Teinture de Vanille.

Vanilla cut fine	15 grm.
Alcohol (85°)	1 l.

Macerate for 14 days, filter, or proceed as follows :

Mexican vanilla......................	15 grm.
Sugar	500 grm.

Triturate the vanilla, cut in fine pieces, with the sugar. Heat the mixture on a water bath with 1 l. of alcohol. Let it cool and filter.

Compound Tinctures.

Preparations of this kind are seldom prepared by liquor manufacturers, as it is easier to mix the simple tinctures, but the product is not as good.

Compound Tincture of Absinthe.
Teinture d'Absinthe Composée.

Absinthe (large) dry	60 grm.
Absinthe (small) dry.................	60 grm.
Cloves........................	6 grm.
Sugar........	30 grm.
Alcohol (60°).............	1 l.

Bruise the cloves and the herbs. Macerate for 8 hours and filter.

Compound Tincture of Cinnamon.
Teinture de Cannelle Composée.

Cinnamon	30 grm.
Cardamom........	15 grm.
Ginger................................	10 grm.
Pepper	10 grm.
Alcohol (60°).............	5 l. 25 c. c.

Macerate the contused materials for 8 days in alcohol, press and filter.

SECTION V.—SPIRITS.

Under the name of spirits our author includes tinctures prepared from the fresh plants. The general method of preparation is as follows : The contused materials are saturated with 90° alcohol. Macerate for 8 days, after which decant the liquid. Filtration is necessary.

Spirit of Angelica.
Alcoolature d'Angélique.

Fresh angelica roots, stems.....	350 grm.
Alcohol (85°)	2 l.

Cut the plant up fine, macerate for 6 days with a little alcohol. Pass through fine linen, press the residue lightly with the remainder of the alcohol and allow it to stand for five or six days. Unite the two infusions and filter.

Spirit of Walnut Shells.
Alcoolature de Brou de Noix.

Nuts, not quite ripe....	1 k.
Alcohol (85°).............	1 l. 25 c. c.

Detach the nuts and pile up with care and allow them to blacken for twenty-four hours. Then macerate in alcohol for two months. Express and filter.

Spirit of Currants.
Alcoolature de Cassis.

Currants ripe and picked from the
  bunch............................ ....   12 k.
Alcohol ....   12 l.

Macerate for 15 days, draw off 4 l. (first infusion),
filter. Treat the residue with 4 l. of alcohol (85°), agitate and mix. At the end of 15 days of maceration,
draw off anew 4 l. (second infusion) and filter. Add to the
remainder 4 l. of alcohol (85°), mix and macerate for
15 days. Draw off all the liquid which constitutes the
third infusion and filter. The residue, after pressing,
constitutes the fourth infusion.

Spirit of Lemon.
Alcoolature de Citron.

Fresh lemon skins .. ..   500 grm.
Alcohol (85°)........... ....   1 l.

Macerate for eight days and filter.

Spirit of Strawberries.

Ripe strawberries....................   1 k.
Alcohol (85°).... ....   1 l.

Macerate for 15 days and filter. In the same manner
are prepared spirit of raspberries, pineapple, etc.

SECTION VI.—DISTILLED WATERS.

Distilled waters, called also in French *hydrolats*,
are the result of the distillation of plants with ordinary water. They are often a by-product in the
manufacture of essences by distillation. The fresh
plants are used wherever possible. They are submitted
to a maceration of some hours, after which they are distilled by steam or the naked fire. A sufficient quantity
of water should be used to cover the materials during
the entire operation, and as the essences for the most
part are not volatilized completely at 100° (C.), it is
often necessary to add salt to the water to raise the
boiling point.

The water and the plants are placed in a still and
heated gradually, so as not to overheat. If the plants
have only a little odor, it is necessary to redistill the
product, that is to say, to submit the product to one
or more distillations with a new supply of the plants.

The principal distilled waters used in the preparation of liquors are :

1. Waters distilled from the flowers of acacia rose, camomile, lily, lily of the valley, orange flowers, violets, elder flowers, etc.

2. Waters distilled from the flowering tops of balm mint, hyssop, lavender, ground ivy, marjoram, melilot, origanum, parsley, rosemary, sage, thyme, etc.

3. Waters distilled from leaves of the cherry laurel, peach, tea and the odorous leaves of the plants of the *labial* family.

4. Waters distilled from the fruits of apricots, bananas, cherries, quinces, strawberries, raspberries, peaches, prunes, cacao, coffee, cloves, musk, maize, green nuts, etc.

5. Waters distilled from the rinds of oranges, lemons, bergamot, etc.

6. Waters distilled from the kernels or stones of apricots, bitter almonds, cherries, peaches, prunes, etc.

7. Waters distilled from the grain and seeds of anise, angelica, Chinese anise, cardamom, caraway, coriander, fennel, juniper, parsley, etc.

8. Waters distilled from the bark or skin of the cinnamon, cascarilla, sassafras, etc.

9. Waters distilled from sandal wood, *lignum vitæ*, etc.

10. Waters distilled from calamus, angelica, ginger root, etc.

The general method of preparation is as follows: The flowering tops are cut up ; the fruits pulped, with their seeds or kernels ; the skins or rinds are contused in a mortar ; the roots, seeds, etc., are crushed ; the wood and tough roots are rasped. The materials which have been thus treated are macerated with 2·5 per cent. of salt and four times their weight of cold water for twenty-four hours. After this time the mass is thrown into a still and submitted to distillation.

The following are examples of distilled waters :

Absinthe Water.
Eau Distillée d'Absinthe.

Top leaves and stems of the absinthe .   1 k.
Salt.................... .... 25 grm.
Water... ....   1 l.

Distill so as to obtain 1 l.

In the same manner the balm mint, marjoram, origanum and the rose are distilled.

Acacia Rose Water.
Eau Distillée d'Acacia Rose.

Fresh flowers of the acacia rose.	1 k.
Salt.	25 grm.
Water.	4 l.

Product, 2 l.

In the same manner the following distilled waters are produced : Violet, lily and lily of the valley, fresh flowering tops of the hyssop, lavender, ivy, melilot, balm mint, sage, thyme, etc. Also the following : Orange, bitter almond, apricot, cherries, peaches, prunes, anise, Chinese anise, caraway, fennel, juniper, etc.

Anise Water.
Eau Distillée d'Aneth.

Dry anise seeds	1 k.
Salt	50 grm.
Water	8 l.

Product, 4 l.

In the same manner are prepared the distilled waters of angelica, coriander, parsley, etc.

Coffee Water.
Eau Distillée de Café.

Browned coffee	1 k.
Water	13 l.

Cinnamon Water.
Eau Distillée d'Ecorce de Cannelle.

For the bark of cinnamon and for roots and woods in general, take :

Material	1 k.
Salt	400 grm.
Water	16 l.

Distill twice, so as to obtain 8 l.

Water of Lemon Peel.
Eau Distillée de Zestes de Citron.

For distilled water from the skins of lemons, oranges, bergamot, etc., take :

Material	1 k.
Salt	100 grm.
Water	20 l.

Product, 10 l.

Distilled Water from the Pulp of Fruits.
Eau Distillée de Fruits Pulpeux.

Pulp of fruits........................... 1 k.
Water.. .... 4 l.
Product, 2 l.

Cherry Laurel Water.
Eau Distillée de Laurier-Cerise.

Leaves of the cherry laurel cut fine.... 1 k.
Salt ......- · .... 50 grm.
Water. .... 1 l.
Product, 1 l.

In the same manner distilled waters are prepared from the leaves of the apricot, cherry and peach trees.

Distilled Water of Tea.
Eau Distillee de Thé.

Tea. .... 1 k.
Water.... .... 20 l.
Product, 10 l.

SECTION VII.—INFUSIONS, DECOCTIONS, AND MACERATIONS.

Infusions are prepared by throwing boiling water upon the plants or other materials to be treated, and as soon as the liquid is charged with the aromatic principle it is removed from the solid residue.

Decoctions are prepared by boiling the material to be treated for a certain time in water. Digestion is the name given to the action of the liquid which is allowed to act upon the material for a certain length of time at a temperature of from 35° to 60° C.

Maceration is an infusion made with a cold liquid. The operation is continued for the time necessary to dissolve the aromatic principles which the materials contain.

SECTION VIII.—JUICES.

The juices of fruits and vegetables are used in the manufacture of sirups and in a number of liquors which have sirups for bases. Juices are extracted from the leaves, fruits, stems, roots, and seeds of plants by a very simple process. The material is pulped in a mortar and submitted to pressure. A small hand press (Fig. 37) is usually used.

Clarification of Juices.—The juices when they come from the press must be clarified. The operation is performed in several ways, but heat is generally used.

Clarification by Fermentation.—This method of clarification is based on the transformation of sugar into alcohol by fermentation, which insures also the preservation of the juice. The juices are placed where the temperature varies from 20° to 25° C. until it is transformed into wine. Forty-eight hours is usually suffi-

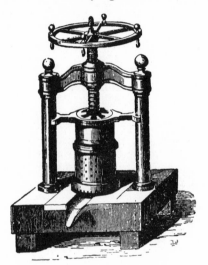

FIG. 37.—HAND PRESS.

cient. When the fermentation is finished, the liquid is filtered.

Clarification by Filtration.—This process is by no means perfect, because there are a number of soluble materials which will bring about changes in the liquid later.

Clarification by Heat.—The juices are heated to about 80° or 90° C. and a solution of white of egg is added. The juice is then skimmed and filtered.

Clarification by Tannin.—M. N. Basset highly recommends the process of clarification which uses a 10 per cent. solution of tannin, which eliminates the albumen.

Preservation of the Juice.—The juices are preserved in heavy bottles.

1. Preservation with Sulphur.—The bottles are filled

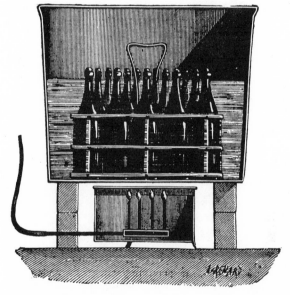

FIG. 38.—APPARATUS FOR HEATING SIRUPS.

and a space equal to two fingers is left between the top of the liquid and the mouth of the bottle, and a piece of candle wick dipped in sulphur is burned in the neck of the bottle.

2. Preservation by the Appert Method.—This is the most convenient method of preserving juices. The clarified juices are bottled in stone or glass bottles and

corked and wired ; they are then carried in a rack to a hot water kettle (*bain marie*) of sufficient size to allow the liquid to cover the bottles (Fig. 38). The water is carried to the boiling point, and after a few seconds the source of heat is removed and the water is allowed to cool down, when the bottles are removed.

The following are receipts :

Juices of Huckleberries, Barberries, Cherries and Grapes.—Crush the fruit and pass the pulp through a horse hair sieve ; crush the marc and unite and carry to the cellar. After 24 hours of fermentation, filter and preserve. The juice of cherries is better when a mixture of black and red cherries is used.

Orange and Lemon Juice.—Remove skin and seeds, crush the pulp and press, and mix with rye straw, washed and cut fine, to assist the separation of the juice. Clarify by repose, filter and preserve.

Quince, Apple and Pear Juice.—Peel and rasp the fruit, taking care not to touch the seeds. Press the pulp, mixed with rye straw, washed and cut fine. Clarify by repose, filter and preserve. The quinces should be fully ripe.

Raspberry Juice.—Crush the fruit and press the marc. The liquid is allowed to repose for one or two days, after which it is filtered. One-fifth the weight of red cherries is sometimes added to the raspberries.

Pomegranate Juice.—Remove the skin and hard partitions. Pulp with the hand and press. Let the juice clear by repose, filter and preserve.

Gooseberry Sirup.—Squeeze the pulp through a horse hair sieve and press. Let the juice repose for 48 hours, filter and preserve. One-fifth by weight of cherries can be added if desired.

Peach, Apricot and Prune Juice.—Clean and pit the fruit, crush the pulp and mix with rye straw, washed and cut fine. Press and put in the cellar for two days, filter and preserve.

SECTION IX.—SIMPLE SIRUPS.

Before describing the manufacture of liquors it is necessary to describe the substances which form their base and their process of manufacture.

Alcoholic liquors are formed essentially of alcohol, sugar and various aromatic principles and sometimes a coloring matter composed of various substances and

intended to render the liquor agreeable to the eye as
well as the taste.

1. Alcohol and the various aromatic principles have
already been treated. 2. Sugar [as the classification
of sugar in this country is entirely different from that
of France, the section on sugar is omitted]. Only a
good quality of sugar should be used. 3. Glucose is
used only in inferior liquors.

Preparing Sugar.

The various degrees of concentration of sugar are
known under various names in French which have no
meaning when translated, so that the French names
are retained.

Sucre au Lessé.

This is a variety of boiled sugar and is made as follows : Boil the sugar until, when a drop is held between
the fingers, when the fingers are separated they will
be connected by a thread of sugar.

Sucre au Perlé.

Repeat the preceding experiment, using a more concentrated sirup. If the thread is of the same consistence as the sirup, it is said to be *perlé*.

Sucre au Soufflé.

If the concentration is continued, when a little is
dipped up by a skimmer, shaken lightly and blown at
the same time, small bubbles will form. The sugar is
then said to be *soufflé*.

Sucre à la Plume.

Continue to boil, and after dipping the finger in water and then in the sugar, and lastly in water again,
the sugar forms a feather-shaped mass.

Sucre au Casse.

A little later the sugar becomes very thick, and after
dipping the fingers in water, then in the sugar, the
sugar hardens so that it breaks on separating the
fingers.

Sucre au Caramel.

This name is used in English and French to denote

the condition when the sugar under the action of prolonged heat turns yellowish brown and gives off a powerful odor. It is used by confectioners and liquor manufacturers for coloring. [This classification is very crude, and leaves much to be desired.—Ed.]

Simple Sirup.

This solution is one of the most important which the liquor manufacturer has to prepare. The name simple sirup is given to a solution of sugar in water concentrated until it has the density of 1·26 (30° Baume) when it is boiling and 1·32 (35° B.) when cold. This corresponds to 1,000 parts of sugar and 530 parts of water. The sirups of sugar are prepared by heat, in the following manner :

White sugar...................	1 k. 700 grm.
Distilled water........	1 k.

Crush the sugar, put it in a basin with the prescribed quantity of water, heat to the boiling point and filter. Simple sirup is also prepared cold, as follows :

White sugar	1 k. 800 grm.
Distilled water	1 k.

Dissolve the sugar in the water and filter.

Coloring Materials.

Coloring matters are added to liquors to render them agreeable to the eye. They are harmless if non-poisonous materials, such as cochineal, saffron, and caramel, are used. The coloring matters that are considered dangerous to health are the salts of lead, copper, aniline derivatives and certain plants, such as aconite.

Red Colors.
Cochineal.

Boil

Water..........	1 l.
Cochineal, pulverized..........	65 grm.

After boiling ten minutes, add

Pulverized alum................	15 grm.
Powdered cream of tartar......	15 grm.

Continue the boiling until the materials are completely dissolved, let it cool, and add ½ l. of alcohol (85°). Filter through cotton, and place in bottles.

Cudbear.

Cudbear	400 grm.
Alcohol (85°)	1 l.

Macerate for five days, agitate several times a day, decant the liquid, treat in the same manner the residue by using a new quantity of alcohol for the same time; unite the two liquids and filter.

Red Sandal Wood.

Wood rasped	30 grm.
Alcohol	1 l.

Macerate for 24 hours, press and filter. This coloring matter can only be used in those liquors which are unaltered by it.

Brazil Wood.
Bois de Brésil au Bois de Fernambouc.

Brazil wood (fine)	250 grm.
Alcohol (85°)	1 l.

Macerate for four days, press and filter.

Yellow Colors.

Saffron Yellow.

Saffron, pulverized	100 grm.
Water	1 l. 50 c. c.

Boil a portion of the water and pour on the saffron. Cover and leave it to macerate until the infusion is cold ; when cold, press. On the residue throw the rest of the water, preferably at the boiling point, then allow it to cool in a closed vessel ; press and unite the two liquids. Add 750 c. c. of alcohol (85°) and filter. Persian and Avignon berries are also employed to color liquors yellow, mixed together with or without saffron. This produces the best color for Chartreuse.

Caramel.

Heat in a deep round basin 1 k. 400 grm. of molasses until the point of caramelization is reached, stirring constantly. Remove from the fire for a moment and throw in small quantities, with stirring, into ½ l. of water heated to 85°. Filter.

Blue Color.

Indigo Blue.

Dissolve 10 grm. of finely pulverized indigo in 100 grm. of sulphuric acid at 66°. Place the indigo in a glass or stone vessel and add the acid, stirring until dissolved. Dilute with 3 l. of water and neutralize with 120 grm. of finely powdered chalk, stirring with care. The sulphate of indigo remains in solution, while the calcium sulphate is precipitated. After repose, decant and filter. Add to the color 30 per cent. of alcohol (85°).

Violet Color.

The violet color is seldom used. It can be made, however, by an ammoniacal solution of cochineal, or by a mixture of cudbear red and blue.

Green Color.

The green color is obtained by a mixture of blue with yellow; for example, indigo with caramel or saffron, or by means of a solution of chlorophyl in concentrated alcohol. This color is very fine, but has the grave fault of being destroyed very rapidly in liquors of less than 70°.

The plants most generally employed in the manufacture of a green color are dry lemon, balm mint (*mélisse*), infused for eight days in 100 grm. per l. of alcohol (86°), dry nettles and spinach. When it is necessary to prepare a fine solution of chlorophyl a certain quantity of alcohol is carried to the boiling point and it is thrown on the leaves, extracting the coloring principles. The solution can be used at once.

SECTION X.—COMPOUND SIRUPS.

Compound sirups are those which are prepared with several aromatic materials and simple sirup made from sugar.

Preparation of Compound Sirups.—All aromatic materials may serve in their preparation, no matter what their condition may be, whether in the form of juice, waters, essences, spirits, etc. The preparations which may be grouped under this head are very numerous. The following are examples :

Absinthe.
Crême d'Absinthe.

Essence of absinthe....	8 drops.
" " cinnamon....	1 drop.
" " rose	1 drop.
Sugar........................	400 grm.
Alcohol...	500 c. c.
Water...............	500 c. c.

Product, 1 l.

Gum Arabic (*Acacia Arabique*).

Tree (Fig. 39) is 7 to 20 feet in height, roots hard, ligneous and have many ramifications. Trunk straight, brown bark, yellow sap, wood hard.

FIG. 39.—GUM ARABIC.

Leaves alternate, flowers yellow. Fruit long, smooth shell, russet to brown. Seeds round and smooth.

Sirup of Gum Arabic.
Sirop de Gomme Arabique.

Refined sugar....	5 k.
White gum arabic.....	600 grm.
Water	2 l. 900 c. c.
Whites of four eggs.	

Wash the gum and dissolve cold in 600 c. c. of water. When the gum is dissolved, pass the solution through a fine sieve of linen and mix with the boiling sirup, which is preferably clarified. Boil for two or three minutes and pass the sirup through a linen straining bag.

Formula of the Codex.

Gum arabic	500 grm.
Cold water.......................	508 grm.

Stir to effect solution and pass through a blanket and mix with :

Boiling simple sirup............. 4000 grm.

Almonds.
Sirop d'Orgeat (Codex).

Almonds, sweet..........	500 grm.
" bitter..................	150 grm.
White sugar....	3000 grm.
Distilled water	1625 grm.
Water of the orange flower......	250 grm.

Cleanse the almonds, remove the skin and make a paste of them in a Wedgwood mortar with 750 parts of sugar and add little by little 125 parts of water. Dilute the paste exactly with 1,500 parts of water and pass through a linen bag. Take up the residue with a little water, so as to obtain 2,250 grm. of emulsion, in which dissolve, on the *bain marie*, or water bath, the remainder of the sugar. Add the orange flower water to the surface of the sirup when it has cooled, then mix.

Balsam of Tolu.
Sirop de Baume de Tolu (Codex).

Balsam of tolu..................	50 grm.
Distilled water	1000 grm.
Sugar (white) sufficient quantity.	

Digest the balsam of tolu with a small quantity of water for two hours over a covered water bath, stirring frequently. Decant the solution and replace the water by a second portion and proceed as before. Re-unite the product of the two digestions, let it cool and filter through paper. Add the sugar in proportion of 180 parts to 100 parts of liquid. Make a sirup by simple solution in the covered water bath and filter through paper.

Coffee.
Sirop de Café.

Coffee, browned.................	5 k.
Simple sirup.....................	4 k.

Exhaust the coffee by a quantity of boiling water sufficient to obtain 10 l. of infusion. The sirup is boiled until it has lost a quarter of its weight, which is replaced with water to make up for that which has been evaporated. Mix thoroughly and filter.

Camomile.
Camomille Romane.

Small plant (Fig. 40) in tufts, velvety stems, attains a height of 20 inches, leaves alternate, sessile, well separated, flowers yellow center, white body, bitter taste, agreeable balsamic odor.

FIG. 40.—CAMOMILE.

Sirup of Camomile.
Sirop de Camomille (Codex).

Dry flowers of the camomile....   100 parts.
Water .... 1000 parts.
Sugar.... ....   1 k. 900 grm.

Make an infusion with boiling water ; allow the mixture to macreate for six hours, pass through linen,
allow it to repose and add the sugar.   Let it dissolve
in a covered water bath.

In the same manner the sirups of absinthe, hyssop,
etc., are made.

Capillaire (*Adiantum pedatum*).
Capillaire du Canada.

Long stem (Fig. 41), leaves 3 to 5 decimeters long,

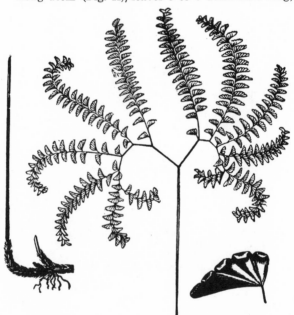

FIG. 41.—CANADIAN CAPILLAIRE.

small leaves of a bright pure green. More aromatic than the capillaire of Montpellier.

Capillaire Sirup.
Sirop de Capillaire.

Fine white sugar...................	5 k.
Canada capillaire.......	250 grm.
Pure water.....................	2 l. 600 c. c.
Whites of four eggs.	

Infuse two-thirds of the capillaire for two hours in 1 l. 800 c. c. of boiling water, add the sugar ; after all has been passed through a sieve clarify with albumenized water. Pour on the boiling sirup to the remainder of the leaves, infuse for two hours and strain through a linen bag.

The sirup of capillaire can be perfumed with the addition of 12½ grm. Pekao tea during the infusion in the boiling sirup. When it is necessary to employ the capillaire of Montpellier, the amount of the capillaire must be increased by one-third.

Cherry Sirup.
Sirop de Cerises.

Refined sugar	5 k.
Conserve of cherries............	2 l. 600 c. c.

Put the filtered conserve in a basin, heat quickly and remove as soon as it boils. Remove from the fire, allow it to rest and skim. Pass through a blanket or filter.

When the sirup is made in the cherry season the conserve is dispensed with and the operation is as follows : Well ripened cherries are stoned and pressed. The juice is allowed to stand 24 hours, then decant and filter. Then the operation is performed as above.

Lemon.
Bichof Froid.

Infuse the skin of a lemon in a glass of *kirsch*. When it has absorbed the perfume remove it and pour the kirsch into 2 l. of white or red wine in which a pound of sugar has been melted.

Raspberry.
Sirop de Framboises.

White sugar	5 k.
Conserve of raspberries	2 l. 600 c. c.

Same operations as in making currant sirup.

Another Receipt.

Sugar............................	5 k.
Ripe raspberries	5 k.

Put the fruits in a copper basin with the sugar and boil until the desired degree of thickness is obtained. Pass through a linen bag.

Sirup of Raspberry Vinegar.
Sirop de Vinaigre Framboise.

White sugar.....................	1 k.
Raspberry vinegar......	500 grm.

Put the sugar in an earthenware vessel, add the sugar, stop up the vessel tight and heat gently over a water bath ; when the sugar is dissolved remove it from the bath, cool off the sirup and bottle.

Raspberry Vinegar.

Fill a jug or crock with ripe raspberries and cover with vinegar. At the end of two months decant the clear liquid and preserve in bottles.

Currant.
Sirop de Groseilles Framboise.

Refined sugar	5 k.
Conserve of currants........... .	2 l. 600 c. c.

Put the sugar in a basin, put on the conserve, heat quickly, stirring constantly. Remove the sirup from the fire and allow it to repose for an instant; skim if necessary. Pass through a filtering bag. Sirup of wild cherry is prepared in the same manner.

Marshmallow.
Sirop de Guimauve.

Refined sugar	5 k.
Dry powdered marshmallow root.	500 grm.

Melt the sugar on a water bath with gentle heat ; keep covered ; when the sugar is entirely dissolved cease the heating and filter, after which the sirup is cooled.

Lemon.
Sirop de Limon.

Refined sugar........	5 k.
Concentrated essence of lemon...	50 c. c.
Citric acid....	40 grm.
Water	2 l. 600 c. c.
Whites of four eggs.	

Cook and clarify the simple sirup, pass through a filtering bag, then add the essence of lemon and the citric acid dissolved in 1 l. of water. Stir briskly, mix, and when cool bottle.

Mulberry.
Mûres.

The black mulberry (Fig. 42) is a tree 25 to 45 feet high, fruit round and plump, red and black.

White sugar..........	5 k.
Mulberries...	5 k.

Take fruit which is not quite ripe, put in a basin

FIG. 42.—BLACK MULBERRY.

with sugar. Carry the mixture to the boiling point or until the sirup is concentrated enough, then pass through a filter.

Walnuts.
Sirop de Noix.

Walnuts....	120 k.
Brandy...........	10 l.

Infuse the green nuts gathered at the end of July in the brandy. Throw in 5 grm. each of cloves, cinnamon, musk and coriander. In December filter the infusion and mix with a sirup prepared with 3 k. 750 grm. of sugar. Leave the mixture for fourteen days, filter and bottle.

Orange Flower.
Sirop de Fleurs d'Oranger.

Refined sugar....................	5 k.
Orange flower water.......	500 c. c.
Water	2 l. 100 c. c.
Whites of four eggs.	

Dissolve the sugar with 1 l. of pure water and 600 c. c. of albumenized water and clarify ; strain, add the orange flower water, mix and cover. Sirup of roses is prepared in the same manner.

Ratafia of Orange Flowers.
Ratafia de Fleurs d'Oranger.

Prepare a bed of orange flowers on a deep plate, then add a layer of fine sugar, then a layer of flowers, and so on, leaving a layer of sugar at the top. Cover and leave in a cool place for 12 hours. Wash the mixture with water and add the alcohol. Leave the liquor for a month, then filter.

To prepare the ratafia the following proportions should be used :

Petals of orange flowers..........	100 grm.
Sugar	750 grm.
Alcohol (85°).......	600 c. c.
Water........	400 c. c.

In the same manner the ratafias of rose, jasmine, etc., are prepared. For the ratafia of acacia flowers it is necessary to employ 1,500 grammes of clean flowers.

Sirup of Orange.
Sirop d'Oranges.

Refined sugar....	5 k.
Concentrated essence of orange..	50 c. c.
Tartaric acid....	80 grm.
Water..	2 l.
Whites of four eggs.	

Same process as that used in making lemon sirup.

Sirup of Orange Peel.
Sirop d'Ecorces d'Oranges (Codex).

Fresh orange peel..............	90 parts.
Water.........	100 parts.

Infuse for 24 hours. Press and dissolve in the infusion, double its weight of sugar.

Bitter Sirup of Orange Peel.
Sirop d'Ecorces d'Oranges Amères (Codex).

Dry peel	100 parts.
Alcohol (60°)	100 parts.
Water..................	1000 parts.

Macerate for 12 hours in alcohol. Throw on all the water in a boiling state and leave the infusion for 6 hours. Press, filter, add 190 parts of sugar to each 100 parts of liquid. The operation should be conducted in a covered water bath.

Punch.
Sirop de Punch au Cognac.

Brown sugar...........	5 k.
Cognac	3 k.
Concentrated essence of lemon...	1 c. c.
Citric acid	6 grm.

The sugar is clarified and cooked to 32° and filtered and put in a vessel with the cognac. The essence of lemon and the citric acid is dissolved little by little. The whole is mixed and the vessel is carefully closed and shaken anew until entirely cold.

Punch au Kirsch.

Refined sugar...	5 k.
Kirsch...........................	2 l. 50 c. c.
Alcohol (85°)....	400 c. c.
Essence of apricot	100 c. c.
Essence of lemon	1 c. c.
Citric acid...........	6 grm.

Same method as that given above.

Rum Punch.
Sirop de Punch au Rhum.

Refined sugar....	5 k.
Rum......................	2 l.
Alcohol (85°)..................... ...	1 l.
Essence of lemon	1 c. c.
Citric acid	6 grm.
Hyson tea...................... ..	25 grm.

Prepare a strong infusion of tea with 400 c. c. of boiling water and add the sirup cooked to 36°. The rest of the operation is the same as before.

Four Fruits.
Sirop des Quatre Fruits.

This name is given to equal parts of the sirups of cherry, strawberry, raspberry and currant.

Tea.
Thé.

The tea plant of China (Fig. 43) attains a height of 3 to 7 feet. Leaves alternate oval, elongated, pointed and of a deep green color. Fruit green and plump. The leaf is the part utilized.

Sirup of Tea.
Sirop de Thé.

The sirup of tea is prepared in the same manner as capillaire sirup, with the following materials :

Tea, Imperial	100 grm.
Tea, Pekao.....................	25 grm.
Pure water....	2 l. 900 c. c.
Whites of fifteen eggs.	

Wash the roots with tepid water; boil them for 20 minutes with 2 l. of water. Pass through a sieve without pressing ; add sugar to the infusion and clarify. To perfume add 25 c. c. of orange flower water.

Vanilla.
Sirop de Vanille.

Vanilla....	60 grm.
Sugar........	500 grm.
Brandy (45°).....................	24 grm.
Water...........................	310 c. c.

Cut the vanilla longitudinally, then transversely as thin as possible. Triturate in a mortar, adding alternately a little sugar and a little brandy to make a homogeneous paste. The mixture is introduced in a vessel with the remainder of the sugar and the water. Dilute the white of an egg with as little water as possible and mix. Place the vessel on a water bath and heat ; at the end of 24 hours strain.

Fig. 43.—CHINESE TEA PLANT.

Violet.
Sirop de Violettes.

Refined sugar..................	5 k.
Fresh flowers, crushed	525 grm.
Water....	2 l. 600 c. c.

Contuse the violets in a mortar put in a tinned water bath. Add 1 l. of water (60° C.) Agitate some time and press the flowers. Put them back in the tin water bath; throw on the rest of the boiling water; infuse for 11 hours; pass through wet linen.

Preservation of Sirups.

Sirups change easily. They ferment or become mouldy. To prevent this loss recourse is had to various systems, of which the best, as it introduces no foreign elements into the liquor, is the Appert process. The bottles of sirup are heated over a water bath to between 60° and 70°, as has been already described for fruit juices.

CHAPTER III.

LIQUORS BY DISTILLATION.

LIQUORS by distillation are obtained from compound perfumed spirits, which are often prepared at the very moment of the manufacture of the liquor. The aromatic materials are cut, sliced, or pulverized, according to their nature, and are submitted to the same treatment as indicated under the head of "Essences." Macerate the materials in alcohol, add the water, and distill, then rectify with another quantity of water, and draw off the finished product. The distillation finished, the treatment with sirup follows, and the liquor is brought up to the desired strength, colored, and clarified. The sugar is always dissolved by heat in the requisite quantity of water, and the sirup is cooled before the mixture with the perfumed spirit. The rest of the water is then added.

The general method of making liquors having been described, the principal receipts for the various liquors will be given.

Absinthe.
Grande Absinthe.

Small plant (Fig. 44), with a strong aromatic odor, taste very bitter, height about twenty inches, leaves white, soft to the touch, yellow flowers.

Ordinary Absinthe.
Absinthe Ordinaire.

Flowering tops and dried leaves of the greater absinthe	250 grm.
Hyssop tops and flowers, dried......	50 grm.
Balm mint.....	50 grm.
Green anise........................	200 grm.

Macerate the materials, which have been lightly pounded, in a water bath with 5 l. 600 c. c. of alcohol (85°). At the end of 24 hours add 5 l. of water, and distill gently, so as to obtain 5 l. 60 c. c. of first quality liquor. Bring up to 10 l. at 46° by the addition of 4 l. 400 c. c. of water, color green with indigo blue, or, better, with chlorophyl. Allow it to repose and decant.

FIG. 44.—ABSINTHE.

Absinthe (*Demi-fine*).

Greater absinthe, flowering tops and leaves...................	250 grm.
Lesser absinthe.................	100 grm.
Hyssop........................	50 grm.
Balm mint	50 grm.
Angelica roots..................	12 grm.
Green anise....................	400 grm.

Cut the materials fine, and macerate with 2 l. 500 c. c. of alcohol (85°). Distill after 24 hours with 2 l. of water. Draw off 2 l. 30 c. c. of good liquor, to which add 3 l. 500 c. c. of alcohol at 85° and 4 l. 200 c. c. of water to obtain 10 l. at 40°. Color as ordinary absinthe.

Absinthe (*Fine*).

Greater absinthe................	250 grm.
Lesser absinthe	50 grm.
Hyssop........................	100 grm.
Balm mint.....................	100 grm.
Green anise....................	500 grm.
Chinese anise..................	100 grm.
Fennel........................	200 grm.
Coriander.....................	100 grm.

Macerate with 5 l. 500 c. c. of alcohol (85°). At the end of 24 hours add 2 l. 750 c. c. distilled water. Draw off 2 l. 750 c. c., add 2 l. 750 c. c. of alcohol at 85° and 2 l. of water to obtain 10 l. at 65°. Color green by the use of indigo blue, caramel, or, better, by chlorophyl.

Absinthe of Pontarlier.
Absinthe de Pontarlier.

Greater absinthe, dry and clean	250 grm.
Green anise..................	500 grm.
Fennel	500 grm.
Alcohol 85°....................	9 l. 500 c. c.

Macerate the plants in alcohol for 12 hours, and add 4 l. 500 c. c. of water before distilling. Draw off 9 l. 500 c. c. of perfumed spirits. Continue the operation until all the phlegm is drawn off, which is set aside for another operation.

The green color of the liquor is imparted by the following:

Small absinthe, dry and clean..	100 grm.
Hyssop, dry tops and flowers.. .	100 grm.
Balm mint (lemon balm)	50 grm.
Perfumed spirit from the previous operation.............	400 c. c.

The small absinthe is cut fine; the hyssop and the balm are powdered in a mortar, and the whole is digested by gentle heat with the spirit in a water bath. The heating operation terminated, the cooled liquid is passed through a haircloth sieve. To the colored liquor add 5 l. 500 c. c. of perfumed spirit, and reduce the strength to 74° by adding 500 c. c. of water, so as to obtain 10 l.

Absinthe of Montpellier.
Absinthe de Montpellier.

Large absinthe, dry............	250 grm.
Green anise	600 grm.
Fennel	400 grm.
Coriander.......................	100 grm.
Angelica seed	50 grm.
Alcohol (85°)	9 l. 500 c. c.

The process is the same as the above, and the coloration is produced by using the following plants:

Dried hyssop.........	75 grm.
Dried balm	75 grm.
Small absinthe	100 grm.

Absinthe of Lyons.
Absinthe de Lyon.

Large absinthe, dried.	300 grm.
Green anise.	800 grm.
Fennel	400 grm.
Angelica seeds.....	50 grm.
Alcohol (85°)	9 l. 500 c. c.

Coloring is made as follows:

Lemon balm	100 grm.
Small absinthe, dried..........	100 grm.
Hyssop dried with flowers.......	50 grm.
Dried veronica	50 grm.

Absinthe of Fougerolles.
Absinthe de Fougerolles.

Green anise..........	750 grm.
Fennel	410 grm.
Large absinthe, clean...........	260 grm.

The color is obtained from the following plants :

Lemon balm................. ...	75 grm.
Hyssop	60 grm.
Small absinthe...	66 grm.
Veronica	66 grm.
Alcohol (85°).	9 l. 500 c. c.
Water.......	5 l.

Macerate in alcohol for 12 hours, add the water at the moment of distillation. Draw off 9 l. 500 c. c. Continue the distillation until all the phlegm has been distilled off. Reduce the strength of the liquid to 74°.

Absinthe of Besançon.
Absinthe de Besançon.

Large absinthe, cleaned.	400 grm.
Green anise.......	500 grm.
Fennel	660 grm.
Coriander.....................	66 grm.

Color with :

Balm...	50 grm.
Small absinthe....	100 grm.
Hyssop.................	83 grm.
Alcohol (85°)	9 l. 500 c. c.
Water.......................	5 l.

Same operation as above.

Absinthe of Nimes.
Absinthe de Nimes.

Large absinthe, cleaned	366 grm.
Green anise...................	366 grm.
Fennel..........	250 grm.
Coriander.........	40 grm.
Roots black alder	25 grm.
Angelica root...........	25 grm.

Color with :

Small absinthe	80 grm.
Hyssop....................	75 grm.
Balm (lemon).....	25 grm.
Veronica.................... ...	40 grm.
Mint..	40 grm.
Alcohol (85°).................. .	9 l. 500 c. c.
Water.............	5 l.

Same operation as given above.

Swiss White Absinthe.
Absinthe suisse blanche.

Large absinthe, cleaned.....	275 grm.
Small absinthe, clean...........	112 grm.
Hyssop flowers.................	110 grm.
Veronica.......................	55 grm.
Genipi (*Artemisia rupestris*)....	55 grm.
Camomile......................	25 grm.
Green anise................	525 grm.
Fennel (Florentine)	525 grm.
Coriander.... ·	100 grm.
Angelica seeds........	55 grm.
Alcohol (85°)..................	9 l. 600 c. c.

Macerate the plants and proceed in the same manner as for green absinthe ; reduce to 74°.

Vulnerable Elixir (Revulsive).
Elixir vulnéraire révulsif.

Take 100 grm. of the dry leaves of each of the following plants :

Absinthe.................	52 grm.
Angelica........................	52 grm,
Basilic	52 grm.
Calamint........................	52 grm.
Fennel.........................	52 grm
Hyssop	52 grm.
Lavender.......	52 grm.
Marjoram	52 grm.
Melilot...................... ..	52 grm.
Balm........... ... .·......	52 grm.
Mint............................	52 grm.
Origanum......................	52 grm.
Rosemary............	52 grm.
Rue...	52 grm.

Savory........................	52 grm.
Sage..........................	52 grm.
Creeping thyme................	52 grm.
Alcohol (85°)..................	5 l.
White sugar	2 k. 500 grm.

Distill and rectify twice. Bring the volume to 10 l. with water.

Human Balsam.
Baume humain.

Balsam of Peru................	15 grm.
Absinthe......................	15 grm.
Coriander.....................	18 grm.
Acacia nuts	125 grm.
Peel of three lemons.	

Divide and break up the materials, macerate for five days in 3 l. of alcohol (85°). Add 2 l. of water, and distill so as to obtain 3 l. Make a sirup with 1 k. 400 grm. of sugar and ¾ of a l. of alcohol, mix cold with the perfumed spirit. Color a light violet.

Swiss Formula for Same.

Large absinthe................	1,000 grm.
Small absinthe................	500 grm.
Angelica root.................	62 grm.
Sweet flag	62 grm.
Dittany (*Dictaine*)	15 grm.

Macerate for eight hours with 6 l. of alcohol (85°), and distill so as to obtain 5 l. Perfume with 4 grm. of essence of green anise. Color olive green.

German Formula.

Large absinthe................	230 grm.
Angelica root	75 grm.
Green anise...................	375 grm.
Star anise....................	150 grm.
Fennel........................	375 grm.
Coriander.....................	110 grm.

Macerate for 48 hours or less with 10 l. of alcohol at 60°. Distill slowly so as to draw off 7½ to 8 l. of the product, and make up to 10 l. at 75° with 90° alcohol. Color green.

Cream of Absinthe.
Crême d'absinthe.

Leaves and flowering tops of large absinthe	250 grm.
Small absinthe.................... ..	60 grm.
Peppermint, dry leaves...	60 grm.
Green anise	60 grm.
Fennel	25 grm.
Sweet flag.....	15 grm.
Skins of two lemons.	

Macerate for two days in 4 l. of alcohol (85°), add 3 l.

FIG. 45.—ANGELICA ROOT.

500 c. c. of water, and draw off 3 l. 800 c. c., add a cold sirup made with 5 k. 500 grm. of sugar and 2 l. 500 c. c. of water.   Dissolve with heat.   Bring up to 10 l. with water, color green and filter.

Amber Seed.
Huile des créoles.

Musk	12·5 grm.
Cloves.........................	12·5 grm.
Amber seed	50 grm.
Alcohol (85°)...................	4 l.
White sugar...................	5 k. 500 grm.

Usual method.   Do not rectify.   Raise to 10 l., color with cochineal.

FIG. 46.—GREEN ANISE.

Angelica.
Angélique.

The roots and twigs of the angelica (Fig. 45) have a musk-like odor, vermicular root, height three to six feet, leaves large, green, and white, flowers greenish yellow.

Cream of Angelica.
Crème d'angélique.

Angelica roots............................	130 grm.
Angelica seeds...........................	125 grm.
Fennel	12 grm.
Coriander................................	15 grm.

Same method as for *crème d'absinthe.*

Green Anise.
Anis vert.

Annual plant (Fig. 46) has many branches, flowers white to red, fruit green, ovoid and striated, of strong odor, stinging taste.

Oil of Anise.
Huile d'anis.

Green anise...........................	200 grm.
Cacarilla (wood).......................	50 grm.
Rosewood..............................	50 grm.

Macerate for 24 hours in 4 l. of alcohol (85°), after having crushed and rasped the wood and the seeds. Distill with 2 l. of water so as to draw off 4 l. Add, when cold, a sirup made with 5 k. 1,500 grm. of sugar in 2 l. 500 c. c. of water. Color red with cochineal.

Star Anise.
Anis etoilé.

THE anise of Japan and China (Fig. 47) is always green; it has a dry fruit, star-shaped, brownish red, aromatic and bitter taste, odor of anise, seeds egg-shaped, smooth, reddish, containing a white and oily kernel.

Ordinary Anisette.
Anisette ordinaire.

Star anise..............................	125 grm.
Bitter almonds, crushed	125 grm.
Florentine orris root in powder.......	62 grm.
Coriander..............................	125 grm.

Contuse the materials and macerate in 4 l. 250 c. c. of alcohol (85°) for eight hours. Add 2 l. of water and distill to obtain 4 l. Add when cold a sirup prepared with 3 k. of sugar and 2 l. of distilled water. Bring up to 10 l. with water, then filter.

Anisette of Bordeaux.
Anisette de Bordeaux.

Green anise........................	160 grm.
Star anise.....	65 grm.
Coriander.	15 grm.
Fennel.......	15 grm.
Hyson tea.	30 grm.

Same treatment and same quantity of product as the preceding preparation.

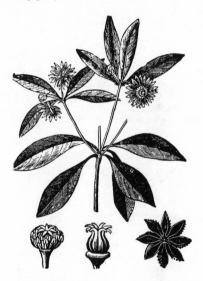

FIG. 47.—STAR ANISE.

Eau-de-vie d'Andaye.

Star anise......	62 grm.
Coriander........	85 grm.
Florentine orris (powdered)......	125 grm.
Skins of six oranges.	
Alcohol (85°)	3 l. 800 c.c.
White sugar...	q. s.

Macerate for eight days. Distill over a water bath without rectifying. Color with caramel.

Product : 10 l.

Cacao (*Theobroma cacao*).
Cacao.

The cacoa tree attains a height of from 10 to 40 feet ; the wood is frail and light ; the flowers are small, reddish, and grow directly from the trunk and the larger branches, as well as from the twigs. The fruit is a kind of bean about the size of a lemon, ovoid and elongated in form ; the surface is broken up by ten longitudinal grooves.

Cacao Oil.
Huile de cacao.

Cacao.........	500 grm.

Heat and pulverize ; then macerate for forty-eight hours with 4 l. 250 c. c. of alcohol (86°). Add 2 l. of water and distill so as to obtain 4 l. 250 c. c. of water ; rectify with 2 l., so as to obtain 4 l. Add a sirup made with :

Sugar	5 k. 500 grm.
Water.........	2 l.

Bring up the volume to 10 l. and filter.

Coffee.
Crême de moka.

Mocha coffee	500 grm.
Bitter almonds, crushed........	100 grm.
Alcohol (85°)....	4 l. 250 c. c.
White sugar......	5 k. 600 grm.

Brown the coffee ; grind and macerate for 24 hours in the alcohol and distill. Rectify the infusion so as to obtain 4 l. and bring the volume up to 10 l.

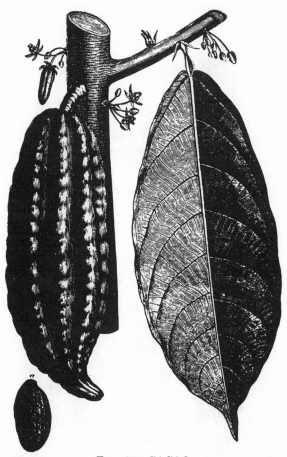

FIG. 48.—CACAO.

Cinnamon (Ceylon).
Cannelle de ceylan.

This comes (Fig. 49a) in the form of roots of bark;
color reddish yellow or fawn; agreeable taste.

FIG. 49.—CINNAMON BARK. (NATURAL SIZE.)
A, Ceylon cinnamon; a, transverse section; B, Chinese
cinnamon; b, transverse section.

Chinese Cinnamon.—Bark thicker than the Ceylon cinnamon (Fig. 49 B*b*); deeper color; odor less agreeable; warm and burning taste.

Cinnamon Oil.
Huile de cannelle.

Ceylon cinnamon..	80 grm.
Chinese cinnamon.......	25 grm.
Cloves...........	5 grm.

Pile up the aromatic materials and macerate for 48 hours in 85° alcohol. Add 2 l. of distilled water, and draw off 4 l. of the product, to which is added a sirup, mixed cold, made from 5 k. 500 grm. of sugar and 2 l. of water. Bring up the volume to 10 l., color yellow with caramel and filter.

Oil of Cedrat.
Huile de cédrat.

Skins of 16 fresh citrons.

Macerate for 24 hours with 5 l. of alcohol at 85°. Distill with 2 l. of water, so as to obtain 5 l. of liquid. Add a sirup made according to the directions given above. Bring the volume up to 10 l. Color golden yellow with caramel and filter.

Parfait amour.

Grated skins of cedrats....	62 grm.
Grated skins of lemons.........	31 grm.
Cloves	4 grm.
Alcohol (60°).......	6 l.
White sugar...................	2 k. 500 grm.

Macerate for two days; distill over a water bath without rectification. Product 10 l.; color with orchil.

Celery.
Crême de céleri.

Celery seed...............	250 grm.
Seeds of doucus of Crete.... ...	12 grm.

Grind the seeds; macerate for two days in 4 l. of alcohol (85°). Add 2 l. of water, and distill to obtain 3 l. 800 c. c. Bring the volume up to 10 l. and filter.

Chartreuse, Benedictine and Trappestine.

The formulas of the three varieties of chartreuse are kept absolutely secret by the monks, but the following are imitations which approach it.   Owing to the number of ingredients, only an expert liquor manufacturer can produce even a passable article, and the beginner's attempts will probably end in failure.

1. Green Chartreuse.
Chartreuse verte.

Chinese cinnamon	1·5 grm.
Mace	1·5 grm.
Lemon balm, dried............	50 grm.
Hyssop in flower tops..........	25 grm.
Peppermint....................	25 grm.
Thyme.................	3 grm.
Costmory	12·5 grm.
Genepi............	25 grm.
Arnica flowers....	1 grm.
Popular balsam buds..........	1·5 grm.
Angelica seeds..................	12·5 grm.
Angelica roots..................	6·5 grm.
Alcohol (85°).......	6 l. 250 c. c.
White sugar....................	2 k. 500 grm.

2. Yellow Chartreuse.
Chartreuse jaune.

Cinnamon.................... ...	1·5 grm.
Mace.....	1·5 grm.
Coriander....................	150 grm.
Cloves....	1·5 grm.
Socotrine aloes............... ...	3 grm.
Lemon balm....................	25 grm.
Hyssop in flower..........	12·5 grm.
Genepi.......	12·5 grm.
Arnica flowers	1·5 grm.
Angelica seeds.......	12·5 grm.
Angelica root	3 grm.
Cardamom, small...	5 grm.
Alcohol (85°)	4 l. 250 c. c.
White sugar	2 k. 500 grm.

3. White Chartreuse.
Chartreuse blanche.

Chinese cinnamon.............	12·5 grm.
Mace	3 grm.
Cloves.	3 grm.
Nutmeg	1·5 grm.
Tonka bean....................	1·5 grm.

Lemon balm......	25	grm.
Hyssop flowering tops	13·5	grm.
Genepi.	12·5	grm.
Angelica seeds..................	12·5	grm.
Angelica roots..................	3	grm.
Cardamom, small...............	3	grm.
Sweet flag	3	grm.
Alcohol.....	5	l. 25 c. c.
White sugar	3	k. 750 grm.

The aromatic materials are cut or crushed. Macerate all for 24 hours in alcohol. Add water from one-half to two-thirds of the latter. Distill so as to obtain nearly all the alcohol. Add the same quantity of water as the first time. Rectify to obtain the largest quantity of liquor of the best quality. To this is mixed when cold a sirup made by the aid of heat, of sugar and two-thirds its weight of water. Raise the volume to 10 l. Color if necessary, using saffron for the yellow, or Persian berries, with chlorophyl for the green. Allow the liquor to repose, and filter.

Benedictine.
Benedictine.

Imitation of the liquor of the monks of Fécamp.

Cloves...................	2 grm.
Nutmegs....	2 grm.
Cinnamon.....	3 grm.
Lemon balm...................	6 grm.
Peppermint	6 grm.
Fresh angelica roots...........	6 grm.
Genepi (Swiss).................	6 grm.
Sweet flag........	15 grm.
Cardamom, small...............	50 grm.
Arnica flowers..............	8 grm.

Cut and bruise the materials, and macerate for two days in 4 l. of alcohol (85°). Distill after having added 3 l. of water, so as to draw off 4 l., to which is added a cold sirup made with 4 k. of sugar and 2 l. of water. Bring up the volume to 10, color yellow, and filter.

Trappistine.

Large absinthe..	40 grm.
Angelica......................	40 grm.
Mint.....	80 grm.
Cardamom......	40 grm.

Lemon balm... ....   30 grm.
Myrrh........ ....   20 grm.
Sweet flag.......................   20 grm.
Cinnamom.......................   4 grm.
Cloves. ....   4 grm.
Mace.... ....   2 grm.
Alcohol (85°) ....   4 l. 500 c. c.
White sugar.................   3 k. 750 c. c.

Proceed the same as for chartreuse. After two days of maceration, distill and rectify, and color green or yellow.

Cumin.
Eau-de-vie de Dantzig.

Cinnamon (Ceylon).............   25   grm.
Cloves.............................   1·5 grm.
Green anise ....   12·5 grm.
Celery seed ....   12·5 grm.
Caraway seed ....   12·5 grm.
Cumin seed   3   grm.
Alcohol (85°) ....   5 l.
Sugar (white)....... .. ..   2 k. 500 grm.

Usual method, without rectification.
Product, 10 l.

Kummel of Dantzic.

Cumin seeds.................. ....   450 grm.
Coriander.......................   30 grm.
Orange peel ....   15 grm.
Alcohol (80°)....... ....   5 l.   65 c. c.
White sugar........ .. ..   2 k. 500 grm.

Kummel of Breslau.

Cumin seeds ....   450 grm.
Chinese cinnamon.... ....   10 grm.
Fennel ....   15 grm.
Alcohol (80°).....................   5 l.   65 c. c.
White sugar....................   2 k. 250 grm.

Genepi or Genipi.
Crême de génépi des Alpes.

Genepi flowers.....   200   grm.
Peppermint in flower..........   100   grm.
Costmary balsamite   100   grm.
Angelica root....   50   grm.
Galanga......................   12·5 grm.
Alcohol ....   4 l. 25 c. c.
White sugar.. . ...   3 k. 75 grm.

General method, same as for other liquors; color, apple green.

Juniper.
Liqueur de genièvre.

Crushed juniper berries..........	600 grm.
Coriander......	20 grm.
Crushed Florentine orris....	40 grm.
Alcohol (80°).....................	5 l. 650 c. c.
Sugar	1 k. 800 grm.

General method, macerate for 5 days, distill gently, without rectification.

Product 10 l., color olive green.

Balm.
Eau de mélisse des Carmes.

Balm, fresh and in flower (*Melissa officinalis*)	3 k. 500 grm.
Tops of hyssop in flower.........	125 grm.
Tops of marjoram	125 grm.
Tops of romarin..........	125 grm.
Tops of sage.................	125 grm.
Tops of thyme.	125 grm.
Angelica root.......	125 grm.
Coriander.................... ...	125 grm.
Ceylon cinnamon................	60 grm.
Mace.....	15 grm.
Nutmegs...........	45 grm.
Peels of 10 lemons.	
Alcohol (85°).....	11 l.

Macerate for three days, distill over water bath, and add 10 l. of water. Draw off 10 l. of good liquor.

Peppermint.
Menthe poivrée.

The peppermint plant (Fig. 50) has a penetrating odor somewhat resembling camphor; strong taste of mint, reddish stem, height 18 or 20 in., leaves green, flowers purplish.

Crême de Menthe (Fr. and Eng.)

Peppermint.....................	600 grm.
Balm....	40 grm.
Sage	10 grm.
Cinnamon of Ceylon...	20 grm.

Florentine orris root............   10 grm.
Ginger......... ....   15 grm.
Alcohol (80°) ... .   5 l.   30 c. c.
White sugar....... ....   2 k. 250 grm.
Same method of operation as for other liquors.
Product, 10 l.

FIG. 50.—PEPPERMINT.

Maraschino.
Marasquin.

Ripe wild cherries	90 k.
Raspberries	12 k.
Cherry leaves	5 k.

Crush the fruit and ferment; add, before distillation, 750 grm. of peach nuts and 500 grm. of orris; distill gently, so as to draw off all the alcohol; rectify to 85°, and add cold a sirup composed of 1 k. 850 grm. of sugar per l. of perfumed alcohol; raise the volume to 10 l. by adding 3 l. 500 c. c. of alcohol.

Oranges.
Curaçoa.

Rasped skins of....	18 or 20 oranges
Cinnamon (Ceylon)........	4 grm.
Mace....	2 grm.
Alcohol (85°)	5 l.
White sugar	1 k. 750 grm.

Macerate for 14 days, distill over a water bath, without rectification, as has already been described.
Product, 10 l.; color yellow, with caramel.

Bitter Curaçoa.

Green anise.... ... ...,.	40 grm.
Juniper berries.........	40 grm.
Orange peel, sour and dry.......	40 grm.
Sage	40 grm.
Large absinthe.......	40 grm.
Sweet flag....	40 grm.
Cloves	20 grm.
Peppermint....	20 grm.
Lavender flowers.	20 grm.
Angelica	20 grm.

All the plants, which must be in a dry state, divided and contused, are macerated for two days with 5 l. 500 c. c. of alcohol, 80°; distill after having added 3 l. of water and drawing off 5 l., then add a cold sirup made from 1 k. 750 grm. of sugar dissolved in 3 l. of water; bring up the volume to 10 l., color with caramel and filter.

CHAPTER IV.

Liquors Made by Infusion.

THIS method of preparation is applied to some sub stances where it is impossible to extract the perfume by distillation with either alcohol or water. Almost all the liquors made by infusion are known under the name of ratafias; this term is applied very loosely. In all the following receipts the ingredients are given on the basis of 10 l. of alcohol, unless otherwise stated.

SECTION I.—ORDINARY LIQUORS.

Ratafia of Black Currant.
Ratafia de cassis.

Infusion of black currants (first)	2 l.	500 c. c.
Alcohol (85°)	1 l.	200 c. c.
Sugar	1 k.	250 grm.
Water	5 l.	400 c. c.

If a second infusion is desired, take the following :

Infusion of currants (second)	3 l.	200 c. c.
Alcohol (85°)		600 c. c.
Sugar	1 k.	250 grm.
Water	6 l.	400 c. c.

And for the third infusion take

Infusion of cassis (third)	3 l.	200 c. c.
Alcohol (85°)		700 c. c.
Sugar	1 k.	250 grm.
Water	3 l.	900 c. c.

In case there is not sufficient perfume, add two or three c. c. of essence or an infusion of the leaves of cassis, diluted with an equal quantity of alcohol.

Quince.
Ratafia de coings.

Expressed juice of ripe quinces		600 c. c.
Essence of cloves		50 c. c.
Alcohol	2 l.	500 c. c.
Sugar	1 k.	250 grm.
Water	6 l.	

Color clear yellow, with caramel.

Raspberry.

In*usion of raspberries...	1 l. 500 c. c.
Infusion of cassis....	500 c. c.
Alcohol (85°)....	1 k. 200 grm.
Sugar...	1 k. 250 grm.
Water....	5 l. 900 c. c.

Walnut.
Brou de noix.

Infusion of old walnut shells....	2 l. 100 c. c.
Essence of nutmeg....	25 c. c.
Alcohol...................	1 l. 300 c. c.
Sugar	1 k. 500 grm.
Water.........................	5 l. 700 c. c.

Color with caramel.

Vanilla.
Huile de vanille.

Infusion of vanilla..	100 c. c.
Tincture of *storax calimite*......	25 c. c.
Alcohol....	2 l. 400 c. c.
Sugar.........................	1 k. 250 grm.
Water..................	6 l. 600 c. c.

Color with orchol.

SECTION II.—DOUBLE LIQUORS.

Cassis.
Ratafia de cassis.

Infusion of cassis (first)....	5 l.
Alcohol (85°)........	2 l. 400 c. c.
Sugar.......	2 k. 500 grm.
Water....	1 l.

Walnuts.
Brou de noix.

Infusion of walnut shells........	4 l. 200 c. c.
Essence of nutmegs.............	0 l. 50 c. c.
Alcohol (85°).......	2 l. 500 c. c.
Sugar.........................	2 k. 500 c. c.
Water........	1 l. 800 c. c.

Color with caramel.

Vanilla.
Huile de vanille.

Infusion of vanilla............... 200 c. c.
Alcohol (85')..................... 4 l. 800 c. c.
Sugar....... . ... 2 k. 500 grm.
Water ... ... 3 l. 300 c. c.
Color with orchol.

SECTION III.—LIQUORS (*Demi-Fines*).

Ratafia of Cherries.
Ratafia de cerises.

Infusion of cherries .... 3 l.
Infusion of wild cherries .... 500 c. c.
Essence of apricot kernels .. .... 500 c. c.
Alcohol..... .... 400 c. c.
Sugar........... . ... 2 k. 500 c. c.
Water........ . ... 3 l. 900 c. c.

Ratafia of Four Fruits.
Ratafia des quatre fruits.

Infusion of cassis (first)........ ... 1 l.
Infusion of cherries .... 1 l.
Infusion of raspberries .... 800 c. c.
Infusion of wild cherry .... 800 c. c.
Alcohol (85°)........ . ... 800 c. c.
Sugar......................... 2 k. 500 grm.
Water...... .... 3 l. 900 c. c.

Vanilla.
Huile de vanille.

Infusion of vanilla.............. 0 l. 400 c. c.
Alcohol (85°).................... 2 l. 200 c. c.
Sugar...................... ...... 2 k. 500 grm.
Water... .... 5 l. 500 c. c.
Color with cochineal.

SECTION IV.—FINE LIQUORS.

Cassis.

Infusion black currants.......... 3 l. 600 c. c.
Infusion of raspberries.......... 800 c. c.
Alcohol (85°)............. .. .... 1 l.
Sugar........ .... 3 k. 750 grm.
Water........................... 2 l. 100 c. c.

Cherry.
Ratafia de cerises.

Infusion of cherries.............	3 l. 500 c. c.
Infusion of wild cherries	800 c. c.
Essence of apricot kernels.......	600 c. c.
Alcohol (85°)....................	400 c. c.
Sugar....	3 k. 750 grm.
Water.......	2 l. 100 c. c.

Walnut.
Brou de noix.

Infusion walnut shells...........	3 l.
Essence of nutmegs.............	35 c. c.
Alcohol........................	1 l. 500 c. c.
Sugar..........................	3 k. 750 grm.
Water.......	2 l. 900 c. c.

Vanilla.
Huile de vanille.

Infusion of vanilla...	800 c. c.
Alcohol (85°):...................	2 l. 400 c. c.
White sugar................	4 k. 375 c. c.
Water........	3 l. 900 c. c.

Color with cochineal.

SECTION V.—SUPERFINE LIQUORS.

Pineapple.
Crême d'ananas.

Pineapples, fresh gathered... ..	800 grm.
Alcohol (85°)....	4 l.

Crush the pineapple and infuse in alcohol for eight days, pass through a silk sieve, throw the crushed sugar into 2 l. 200 c. c. of water, add 50 c. c. infusion of vanilla. Color clear yellow with caramel.

Angelica.
Hygienic Dessert Liquor Formula of Raspail.
Liqueur Hygiénique de dessert (Raspail).

Alcohol (56°)	100	c. c.
Angelica root	3	grm.
Calamus (sweet flag)............	0·2	grm.
Myrrh...........	0·2	grm.
Cinnamon..........	0·2	grm.
Aloes	0·2	grm.

Cloves	0·1 grm.
Vanilla	0·1 grm.
Camphor	0·05 grm.
Nutmegs	0·025
Saffron	0·005

Allow the materials to digest for several days in a well-corked bottle placed in the sun. Strain through a fine cloth and bottle ; keep well corked.

Ratafia of Currants of Dijon.
Ratafia de cassis de Dijon.

Infusion of currants (first)	2 l. 500 c. c.
Infusion of cherries	500 c. c.
Infusion of wild cherries	500 c. c.
Infusion of raspberries	500 c. c.
Bordeaux wine	1 l.
White sugar	5 k.
Water	1 l. 600 c. c.

Ratafia of Cherries of Grenoble
Ratafia de cerises de Grenoble.

Infusion of cherries	2 l. 500 c. c.
Infusion of wild cherries	1 l. 500 c. c.
Essence of apricot kernels	600 c. c.
Essence of raspberries	400 c. c.
White sugar	5 k.
Water	1 l. 600 c. c.

Ratafia of Raspberries.

Infusion of raspberries	3 l.
Infusion of wild cherries	1 l.
Alcohol (85°)	1 l.
White sugar	5 k.
Water	1 l. 600 c. c.

Ratafia of Wild Cherries of Grenoble.

Put in a bright copper vessel 10 k. of wild cherries, ripe and stemmed, heat rapidly and stir with a wooden spatula until the liquid is thick ; then throw the mass in a large vessel and, after cooling, add 5 l. 500 c. c. of white brandy at 59°. Let the mixture infuse six days or less, stirring from time to time ; draw off and let the liquor clarify itself.

Walnuts.
Crême de brou de noix.

Infusion of old walnut shells.....	4 l.
Essence of nutmegs.............	50 c. c.
Alcohol (85°)	1 l.
White sugar	5 k.
Water........................	1 l. 600 c. c.

Pears.
Crême de poires de Rousselets.

This liquor is prepared in the same way as *Creme d'ananas* (Pineapple).

Russet pears, ripe...............	1 l.
Essence of raspberries........	1 l.
Infusion of vanilla..............	0 l. 200 c. c.
Alcohol (85°).................	2 l. 800 c. c.

Vanilla.
Crême de vanille.

Infusion of vanilla	1 l.
Alcohol (85°)....	2 l. 600 c. c.
White sugar	5 k. 500 grm.
Water....................	2 l. 600 c. c.

Color with cochineal.

CHAPTER V.

LIQUORS PREPARED FROM ESSENCES.

LIQUORS are readily prepared from essences; in general the method of manufacture is to dissolve a certain quantity of the essential oil in alcohol, and reduce the solution to the desired degree by the addition of water and sugar if necessary. The quality of liquor prepared by this process depends upon the quantity of water and essential oil and the quality of the alcohol employed. The proportions generally used are as follows for 10 l. of liquor :

	Alcohol.	Sugar.	Water.
Ordinary liquors	2 l. 500 c. c.	1 k. 250 grm.	6 l. 600 c. c.
Demi-fines "	2 l. 800 c. c.	2 k. 500 grm.	5 l. 500 c. c.
Fine..... "	3 l. 200 c. c.	4 k. 375 grm.	3 l. 800 c. c.
Superfine "	4 l.	5 k. 600 grm.	2 l. 600 c. c.

The method generally adopted presents no difficulties. A flask or other glass vessel is carefully cleansed, dried and placed on one of the pans of a balance. The essences are added to part of the alcohol so as to fill the vessel to two-thirds of its capacity. Cork and shake until the essences are completely dissolved. The solution is mixed with the remainder of the alcohol and the whole is briskly shaken. The usual processes of treating with sirup, coloration, clarification, filtration after repose, etc., are conducted as already described.

SECTION I.—ORDINARY LIQUORS.

Liqueurs ordinaires.

Absinthe.
Absinthe ordinaire.

Essence of absinthe..............	0·6 grm.
Essence of English mint.........	0·6 grm.
Essence of green anise...........	3 grm.
Essence of lemon	3 grm.
Essence of fennel.................	0·8 grm.
Alcohol (85°).....................	2 l. 500 c. c.
Sugar..........	1 k. 250 grm.
Water...........................	6 l. 600 c. c.

Color green.

Superfine Absinthe.
Absinthe surfine.

Essence of absinthe	1	grm.
Essence of mint	0·75	grm.
Essence of fennel	0·75	grm.
Essence of green anise	3	grm.
Essence of lemon	3	grm.
Alcohol (85°)	4 l.	
Sugar	5 k.	600 grm.
Water	2 l.	600 c. c.

Cream of Absinthe.
Crême d'absinthe.

Essence of absinthe	15 grm.	
Alcohol (90°)	5 l.	
Sugar	4 k.	500 grm.

Make a sirup with the sugar and one-half its weight of water and cool. Dissolve the essence and mix. Increase the mixture to 10 l., color green and filter.

Angelica.
Eau d'angélique.

Essence of angelica	0·6 grm.	
Alcohol (85°)	2 l.	500 c. c.
Water	6 l.	600 c. c.
Sugar	1 k.	250 grm.

Anisette (Ordinary).

Essence of anise	3	grm.
Essence of star anise	3	grm.
Essence of sweet fennel	0·5	grm.
Essence of coriander	0·05	grm.
Alcohol (85°)	2 l.	500 c. c.
Water	60 l.	600 c. c.
Sugar	1 k.	250 grm.

Anisette (*demi-fine.*)

Essence of anise	3·2	grm.
Essence of star anise	3·2	grm.
Essence of sweet fennel	60	grm.
Essence of coriander	0·05	grm.
Essence of French neroli	0·1	grm.
Alcohol (85°)	2 l.	800 c. c.
Water	5 l.	500 c. c.
Sugar	2 k.	500 grm.

Lemon.
Parfait amour.

Essence of lemon (distilled)... ...	4·5 grm.
Essence of cedrat (distilled)... ...	1·5 grm.
Essence of coriander...............	0·1 grm.
Alcohol (85°)....	2 l. 600 c. c.
Water.........................	6 l. 600 c. c.
Sugar.	1 k. 250 grm.

Color with orchol.

Mint.
Menthe anglaise.

Essence of English mint........	2 grm.
Alcohol (85°)................	2 l. 500 c. c.
Water....	6 l. 600 c. c.
Sugar.......	250 grm.

Crème de menthe.

Essence of English mint..........	3·5 grm.
Alcohol (85°)....	2 l. 800 c. c.
Water........	5 l. 500 c. c.
Sugar..........................	2 k. 500 grm.

Noyau.
Crème de noyau demi-fine.

Essence of noyau	5 grm.
Alcohol.......	2 l. 800 c. c.
Water.........................	5 l. 500 c. c.
Sugar..........	2 k. 500 grm.

Orange.
Curaçao ordinaire.

Essence of curacao.............	4　grm.
Essence of Portugal distilled	1·5 grm.
Essence of cloves	0·2 grm.
Alcohol (85°).....................	2 l. 500 c. c.
Water..	6 l. 600 c. c.
Sugar...........................	1 k. 250 grm.

Color with caramel.

Curaçao (*demi-fine*).

Essence of curacao, distilled... ..	5 grm.
Essence of Portugal	2 grm.
Essence of cloves.........	0·4 grm.
Alcohol (85°).............	2 l. 800 c. c.
Water............	5 l. 500 c. c.
Sugar........................... .	2 k. 500 c. c.

Color with caramel.

Orange Flowers.
Crême de fleurs d'oranger.

Essence of French neroli... ...	1·2 grm.
Alcohol (85°)...	2 l. 800 c. c.
Water	5 l. 500 c. c.
Sugar...	2 k. 500 grm.

Rose.
Huile de rose.

Essence of roses	0·8 grm.
Alcohol (85°)...	2 l. 800 c. c.
Water...	5 l. 500 c. c.
Sugar...	2 k. 500 grm.

Vespétro.

Essence of anise...	3 grm.
Essence of cassis	2 grm.
Essence of sweet fennel...	0·6 grm.
Essence of coriander...	0·8 grm.
Essence of lemon, distilled... ..	1 grm.
Alcohol (85°)	2 l. 800 c. c.
Water...	2 l. 600 c. c.
Sugar...	2 k. 500 grm.

SECTION II.—FINE LIQUORS.
Liqueurs Fines.

Anisette.

Essence of star anise...	5 grm.
Essence of anise...	0·2 grm.
Essence of sweet fennel... ...	0·6 grm.
Essence of coriander...	0·1 grm.
Essence of sassafras...	0·4 grm.
Essence of orris	4 grm.
Essence of ambrette (amber seed).	0·6 grm.
Alcohol (85°)...	3 l. 200 c. c.
Water...	3 l. 900 c. c.
Sugar...	4 k. 375 grm.

Cream of Celery.
Crême de céleri.

Essence of celery	2 grm.
Alcohol (85°)...	3 l. 100 c. c.
Water...	3 l. 900 c. c.
Sugar...	4 k. 375 grm.

Curaçao.

Essence of curacao, distilled......	7　grm.
Essence of Portugal.　.　　......	2·5 grm.
Essence of cloves...　........　....	0·5 grm.
Bitter infusion of curacao, a sufficient quantity.	

Alcohol (85°), sugar and water, same quantities as for anisette.

Eau-de-vie de Dantzig.

Essence of cinnamon (Ceylon)...	0·4 grm.
Essence of cinnamon Cluria......	1·2 grm.
Essence of coriander.......... ..	0·2 grm.
Essence of lemon, distilled　...	2·5 grm.
Essence of Portugal, distilled.. .	0·8 grm.
Alcohol (85°), water and sugar as above.	

Elixir de Garus.

Essence of Chinese cinnamon...	1·2 grm.
Essence of cloves.........	0·6 grm.
Essence of musk.......	0·2 grm.
Socotrine aloes	4　grm.
Saffron...........................	4　grm.
Myrrh..	2·5 grm.

After dissolving the essences, make an infusion of the aloes, myrrh, and saffron for three days in alcohol. Same quantity of 85° alcohol, water and sugar as before. Color with caramel.

Crême de menthe.

Essence of English mint.	5　grm.

Alcohol (85°), water and sugar, same quantities as above.

Eau de sept graines.

Essence of angelica........	0·3 grm..
Essence of anise................ ..	1·5 grm,
Essence of celery.................	0·5 grm.
Essence of coriander	0·1 grm.
Essence of sweet fennel....... ...	0·5 grm.
Essence of Portugal, distilled....	0·5 grm.
Essence of lemon, distilled.......	5　grm.

Alcohol (85°), water and sugar, same proportions as already indicated. Color with caramel.

SECTION III.—SUPERFINE LIQUORS.

Liqueur surfines.

The quantities of alcohol (85°), sugar, and water usually employed in the preparation of superfine liquors are :

Alcohol (85°).....	3 l.
Sugar.......................	5 k. 500 grm.
Water.......	2 l. 600 c. c.

For 10 l.

Cream of Absinthe.
Crème d'absinthe.

Essence of absinthe...............	0·6 grm.
Essence of English mint...........	0·6 grm.
Essence of anise..................	3 grm.
Essence of sweet fennel............	0·8 grm.
Essence of lemon distilled....	3 grm.

Anisette.

Essence of star anise....,..... ...	7 grm.
Essence of anise....	2 grm.
Essence of sweet fennel	0·8 grm.
Essence of coriander..............	0·1 grm.
Essence of sassafras....	0·6 grm.
Extract of orris........	6 grm.
Extract of ambrette...............	0·8 grm.

Crème de Barbades.

Essence of lemon, distilled	6 grm.
Essence of Portugal, distilled......	3 grm.
Essence of cinnamon of Ceylon....	0·4 grm.
Essence of cloves	0·4 grm.
Essence of nutmeg...,......	0·2 grm.

Chartreuse.
Liqueur de la grande Chartreuse.

Essence of lemon balm......... ...	0·2 grm.
Essence of hyssop.......	0·2 grm.
Essence of angelica...............	1 grm.
Essence of English mint....	2 grm.
Essence of Chinese cinnamon......	0·2 grm.
Essence of nutmeg...	0·2 grm.
Essence of cloves	0·2 grm.

Color yellow or green.

Curaçao.

Essence of curaçao, distilled	10	grm.
Essence of Portugal, distilled	4	grm.

Bitter infusion of curaçao a sufficient quantity; color with Pernambuco wood.

Kirschenwasser.
Huile de Kirschwasser.

Essence of noyaux	4	grm.
Essence of French nerole	0·4	grm.

Cream of Orange Flowers.
Crème de fleurs d'orangers.

Essence of French neroli	2	grm.
Orange flower water	0·2	l.

Crème de menthe.

Essence of English mint	6	grm.

Liquor of Mézenc.

Essence of nutmegs	0·2	grm.
Essence of mace	0·2	grm.
Essence of camomile	1	grm.
Essence of daucus	0·5	grm.
Essence of coriander	0·3	grm.
Myrobolans	6	grm.
Ambrette (seed musk)	6	grm.
Vanilla	6	grm.

After the essences are dissolved, infuse the last three substances in alcohol for 15 days; color with Pernambuco wood, add a few drops of a solution of tartaric acid to brighten up the color.

Crème de roses.

Essence of roses	1·5 grm.

Color with cochineal.

Crème de noyaux de Phalsbourg.

Essence of apricot seeds	5	grm.
Essence of bitter almolds	1	grm.
Essence of Portugal, distilled	1	grm.
Essence of lemon, distilled	0·8	grm.
Essence of Chinese cinnamon	0·4	grm.
Essence of cloves	0·2	grm.
Essence of nutmegs	0·1	grm.
Essence of neroli	0·2	grm.

Vespétro de Montpellier.

Essence of anise..................	4	grm.
Essence of caraway	3	grm.
Essence of fennel......	8	grm.
Essence of coriander	0·4	grm.
Essence of lemon, distilled	2	grm.

Anisette de Hollande.

Essence of star anise.............	5	grm.
Essence of anise......	5	grm.
Essence of bitter almonds.........	0·8	grm.
Essence of coriander	0·1	grm.
Essence of fennel	0·2	grm.
Essence of roses...	0·2	grm.
Essence of angelica	0·4	grm.

Alkermès de Florence.

Essence of calamus....	0·3	grm.
Essence of cinnamon, Ceylon	0·2	grm.
Essence of cloves	0·5	grm.
Essence of nutmegs........	0·3	grm.
Essence of roses......	0·4	grm.
Extract of jasmine....	3	grm.
Extract of anise...................	3	grm.

Rosolio de Turin.

Essence of anise	2·5	grm.
Essence of fennel.................	0·3	grm.
Essence of bitter almonds.....	3	grm.
Essence of roses	0·6	grm.
Extract of ambergris	0·4	grm.

Color with cochineal.

Marasquin de Zara.

Essence of noyaux........	3·5	grm.
Essence of neroli....	0·5	grm.
Extract of jasmin.................	1	grm.
Extract of vanilla	1·5	grm.

Crême d'heliotrope.

Extract of heliotrope	18	grm.

Color a clear rose with cochineal.

Crême de jasmin.

Extract of jasmin...............	15	grm.

Color with caramel.

Crême de jonquille.

Extract of jonquille................ 14 grm.
Color with caramel.

Crême de millefleurs.

Essence of neroli	0·5 grm.
Essence of roses....................	0 2 grm.
Extract of jasmin	2 grm.
Extract of jonquille................	1·5 grm.
Extract of heliotrope....	2·5 grm.
Extract of reseda........	2 grm.
Extract of tuberose.....	2 grm.

Crême de réséda.

Extract of reseda... .... 17·5 grm.

CHAPTER VI.

Aromatic Wines and Hydromels.

UNDER the name hydromel are included many drinks which have almost passed out of use, the base of which is honey. These liquors are little used in France, and are principally made and consumed in northern countries. The following is one of the best known receipts :

White honey.......	15 k.
Cream of tartar..................... ...	500 grm.
Elder flowers....	500 grm.
Pressed brewer's yeast...............	500 grm.

Make an infusion of the elder flowers in 100 l. of boiling water, a quarter of an hour afterward add the cream of tartar. When the infusion commences to cool (about 30° C.) add the honey and the yeast ; place all in a vessel having a constant temperature of 18° to 22.° The liquor ferments, and when the effervescence has ceased, draw off the liquor and cork tightly. The elder flower can be replaced with other aromatic substances, such as thyme, rosemary, sage, etc.

Hippocras.

Hippocras was formerly very celebrated, but is rarely used at the present day. The following receipt for white hippocras will suffice, as this liquor is rarely or never made at the present day. The receipt is from *Le Confiseur royal* (1737). Take two pints of good white wine, a pound of sugar, an ounce of cinnamon, a little mace, two grains of white pepper (whole), and a lemon divided into three parts; let the whole infuse some time; run through a filtering bag held open by two little sticks; pass through three or four times. If the liquor does not filter easily, add half a glass of milk, which will produce the desired effect. You can give the odor of musk and ambergris to the hippocras by adding a crushed grain or two to the sugar, or enveloped in cotton and attached to the point of the filter.

Cherries.
Vin de cerises.

Cherries............................ .	25 k.
Currants.......	5 k.

Crush all in a small cask; allow it to ferment for three days, and add 500 c. c. of alcohol (80°); at the end of six days the clear liquid is drawn off, and to each l. 5 k. of sugar are added. The wine is then put in a tun with spices, mace, pepper, cinnamon, coriander, etc., according to taste.

Cider.
Vin de pommes.

A liquor is prepared in the United States which, when old, recalls Rhine wine. It is made by taking ripe apples, pressing and gathering the juice, evaporating to half; when cold add sufficient brewer's yeast to develop a brisk fermentation; after twenty-fours draw off and place in barrels, or, better, bottle.

Vermouth of Turin.
Vermouth de Turin.
Vermout de Torino (Italian).

Large absinthe	125 grm
Gentian	60 grm.
Angelica root	60 grm.
Holy thistle (*Centaurea benedicto*)	125 grm.
Calamus aromaticus	125 grm.
Elecampane	125 grm.
Lesser centaury	125 grm.
Lesser germander	125 grm.
Chinese cinnamon	100 grm.
Nutmegs	15 grm.
Sliced fresh oranges	6 grm.
Sweet wine of Picpoul	95 l.
Alcohol (85°)	5 l.

Infuse or digest for five days, draw off, size with fish glue, allow it to repose for eight days, size again and bottle.

Receipt for Vermouth (Ollivero).

Coriander	500 grm.
Bitter orange peel	250 grm.
Powdered orris	250 grm.
Elder flowers	200 grm.
Cinchona (red)	150 grm.
Calamus	150 grm.
Large absinthe	125 grm.
Holy thistle (*Centaurea benedicto*)	125 grm.
Elecampane	125 grm.

Lesser centaury....................... 125 grm.
Lesser germander................ ...... 125 grm.
Chinese cinnamon.... .... 100 grm.
Angelica roots........................ 60 grm.
Nutmegs............................. 50 grm.
Galanga............................. 50 grm.
Cloves............................. 50 grm.
Cassiæ...................... ... . 30 grm.
White wine of Picardy.............. 100 l.

Infuse for five or six days, size with fish glue, and repose for fourteen days. For a vermouth of the best
quality, add 2 l. of an infusion of toasted bitter almonds and 3 l. of good cognac.

First Quality Vermouth.

Clean absinthe .... 500 grm.
Small absinthe............ .... 500 grm.
Cinchona (red).. .... 500 grm.
Florentine orris............. ... ... 400 grm.
Veronica.... .... 500 grm.
Liverwort. .... 500 grm.
Holy thistle. .... 500 grm.
Elder flowers..................... .. 500 grm.
Rhubarb .... 60 grm.
Ripe orange peel........ ... . 500 grm.
Curaçao peel......... .. .. 125 grm.
Peach stones........... .... 500 grm.
Orange flowers..................... 250 grm.
Semen-contra .. .. 50 grm.
Lesser centaury................ ... 125 grm.
Lesser germander.................. 125 grm.
Cognac (40°)....................... 16 l.
White sugar dissolved in the wine... 6 k.

Infuse for two months, agitate daily for fifteen days,
draw off, size, put the vermouth in bottles. The wine
of Picardy is preferable.

Vermouth au madère.

Large absinthe...................... 125 grm.
Angelica roots.................... .. 60 grm.
Holy thistle....................... 125 grm.
Liverwort......................... 125 grm.
Veronica........ .... 125 grm.
Rosemary........ .... 125 grm.

Rhubarb ....   30 grm.
Cinchona (red) ... .   200 grm.
Powdered orris........... ... ... 250 grm.
Infusion of curaçao.... ... .   25 c. c.
Madeira wine. ....   92 l.
Grape sirup ... . ·· .   3 l.
Cognac (40˝)........................   5 l.

Digest for three days, draw off the clear liquid, size with fish glue; after eight days of repose draw off, size anew, draw and place in bottles.

CHAPTER VII.

MEDICINAL WINES.

THE following aperitives and cordials follow the *Codex*

Absinthe.
Vin d'absinthe.

Dry leaves of absinthe.	30 grm.
Alcohol (60°).... ··	60 grm.
White wine...	1000 grm.

Cut the absinthe and put in immediate contact with the alcohol in a closed vessel, after twenty-four hours draw off, add the wine, allow it to macerate for ten days, and agitate from time to time. Press and filter. This is a bitter wine, and is tonic and stomachic.

Coca.
Vin de coca.

Leaves of coca................. ...	60 grm.
Wine........	1000 grm.

Crush the leaves and macerate in a closed vessel for ten days in wine, agitating from time to time. Press and filter.

The wines of colombo, eucalyptus and bitter quassia are prepared as follows :

Material	30 grm.
Wine.....	1000 grm.

Reduce the root or other material to a coarse powder ; macerate in a closed vessel with the wine for six days, agitating from time to time. Press and filter.

Gentian.

The gentian (Fig. 51) grows to about one meter in height. Large root, large wrinkled leaf, bitter taste, flowers yellow or yellowish red.

Gentian Wine.
Vin de gentiane.

Gentian root, cut fine..............	30 grm.
Alcohol (60°).......................	60 grm.
Red wine.........................	1000 grm.

Place the root in the alcohol in a closed vessel and after twenty-four hours add the wine, macerate for ten days and agitate from time to time. Press and filter. Gentian wine loses its color, so that it should be prepared as wanted.

Quinquina (Quinine).
Vin de quinquina gris.

Quinquina, gray officinal..........	50 grm.
Alcohol (60°)	100 grm.
Red wine	1000 grm.

Reduce the quinquina to a coarse powder, leave it in contact with alcohol for 24 hours in a closed vessel, add the wine, macerate for ten days and agitate from time to time. Press and filter.

In the same manner are prepared the yellow and the red wine of quinquina, but in making them take 25 grm. of quinquina for the same quantity of alcohol and wine. White wine may be substituted for the red wine.

FIG. 51.—GENTIAN.

CHAPTER VIII.

PUNCHES.

UNDER this name are included mixtures composed of an infusion of tea, lemon juice, brandy, rum, etc.

Rum Punch.
Punch au rhum.

Prepare an infusion of 10 to 15 grm. of good hyson tea with a half liter of boiling water. Cut up half a lemon and place it at the bottom of a deep vessel, add 200 to 250 grm. of fine sugar and throw on the hot tea. Add one-half liter of old rum carefully, so that it does not mix with the infusion of tea. In a few seconds the rum becomes heated, takes fire and is allowed to burn until it goes out, then mix thoroughly and serve the punch.

Punch au kirsch.

This is prepared in the same manner as brandy or cognac punch.

CHAPTER IX.

THE CLARIFICATION AND THE PRESERVATION OF LIQUORS.

SECTION I.—CLARIFICATION OF LIQUORS.

LIMPIDITY is one of the principal points to be looked at in the manufacture of liquors. This is usually done either by a process called *collage* in French, the English word sizing coming nearly to the meaning, or by filtration.

Sizing.—Various substances serve to size liquors—albumen, white of an egg, fish glue, gelatine, milk, etc. For example, in sizing a hectoliter of liquor with white of egg, the operation is carried on in the following manner:

Take the whites of three eggs, beat in one l. of water, with sprigs of osier or a Dover egg beater, throw into the liquor and allow it to repose from 24 to 48 hours.

This method is largely used for those liquors which are milky, by reason of the minute globules of volatile oil or resinous substances which enter into the composition of the liquor. It can also be used for liquors prepared by infusion, but the quantity of white of egg is reduced to two-thirds.

Fish glue for clarification is used as follows: 10 grm. of fish glue, are dissolved in a small quantity of white wine or water to which a little vinegar is added. Beat from time to time and add a little vinegar or white wine so as to reach 1 l. When dissolved, the fish glue is thrown into the liquor, which is beaten for ten minutes. Allow it to repose for several days. Fish glue answers admirably for those liquors which are very alcoholic.

Gelatine (30 grm.) is dissolved in 1 l. of water, which is heated. Add the solution to the liquor, strongly cork or bung it up and leave it to repose for several days. The gelatine is used principally for white liquors and those weak in alcohol.

The liquors which contain little alcohol are treated with milk. A liter of milk is heated and poured while hot into the liquor. Stop up tightly and add 15 grm. of alum dissolved in a glass of water. Cover closely or bottle and allow it to repose for several days.

Filtration.—Filtration has for its end the removal by means of some substance which will allow only the liquid to penetrate, of particles of matter which are held in suspension. When only a fair amount of fil-

FIG. 52.—FILTERING BAG.

tration is required, that is when the liquid need not be absolutely limpid, a blanket or filtering bag (Fig. 52) is used. To obtain perfectly clear liquor it is necessary to use unsized filter paper, which is usually either

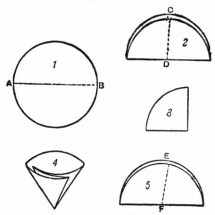

FIG. 53.—FILTER PAPER.

white or gray. In general liquor manufacturers employ round filters, which are folded as follows :

A circular filter paper is readily made to fit the funnel by folding it across one diameter as shown at A B in 1, Fig. 53, then on folding it again at right angles, as at C D in 2, it has the form of 3 ; now, on inserting the finger between the folds of the paper, it may be opened out to the conical shape shown in 4, and is thus ready to place in the funnel. If, however, the paper should not fit well into the cone of the latter, it may be refolded along the line, E F, as in 5, or along any other

FIG. 54.—DOUBLE FUNNEL.

suitable line, and may thus be adapted to suit a funnel constructed with any angle at its apex.

If it be necessary to clear any solution which attacks paper, a plug of spun glass or of asbestos may be lightly rammed into the apex of the funnel, and will form an efficient filtering medium in lieu of paper.

The filter paper is placed in a glass funnel as illustrated in Fig. 54, which shows a pleated filter in position. Liquor manufacturers use large copper funnels. That made by the house of M. Egrot is shown in Fig. 55. It consists of two funnels and a reservoir for the liquor, all controlled by cocks. When large masses

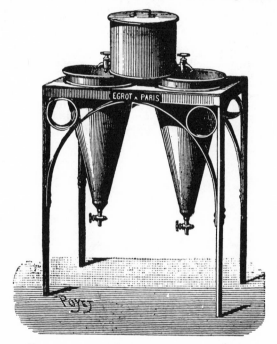

FIG. 55.—MOUNTED FILTERS WITH
RESERVOIRS.

of liquid are to be treated, continuous filters or filter presses are used.

SECTION II.—PRESERVATION OF LIQUORS.

Preservation.—After filtration the liquor should be placed in dry casks and stored in a place which has a constant temperature, and away from the light.

Aging.—Age has the effect of mellowing liquors, by reason of the liquor becoming little by little more intimately mixed. The essential oils also becoming oxidized, this modifies the odor and renders it more agreeable. Aging can only be accomplished with time, and no attempt should be made to arrive artificially at this point.

Mellowing.—Liquor manufacturers use a device for imparting a mellowness to liquors which would ordinarily be only acquired with age. The liquor is heated in a water bath to 60°, a cooling pipe or an ordinary still being used. This temperature reached, the fire is put out and the still is allowed to cool down slowly. Liquors which are to be subjected to this operation must not be colored in advance.

PART III.—PRESERVES.

CHAPTER I.

BRANDIED FRUITS.

BRANDIED fruits are the most important preserves that the liquor manufacturer is called upon to prepare, and their manufacture is now a large industry. To obtain good results the most minute care should be used.

Choice and Preparation of the Fruit.—Fruits which are to be preserved in brandy must be sound and plump. They should be gathered before they are entirely ripe and on no account should any decayed or bruised fruit be used. Dust the fruit carefully with a linen cloth, especially if the fruit has a down, as a peach. This done, the fruit is pricked in several places, so that the alcohol can reach the center. The fruit is then thrown in a tub of cold water, as cold as possible, to render the fruit firm.

Whitening or Bleaching.—This operation has for its end the removal of a part of the acrid taste. It is done by plunging the fruit in a vessel of water heated to about 95°. The vessel is removed from the fire for ten minutes, when it is reheated until the fruit begins to float over the surface of the water. At this moment the fruit is removed and thrown into cold water. The whitening is done very rapidly, and is safe if proper care is used.

The fruit being completely cold, is drained on a horse hair sieve. The fruit is now placed in the brandy, that which marks 53° to 58° being used, according to the kind of fruit, the strongest being used for those fruits which contain the most water. After remaining six days in alcohol, the process of sweetening can begin. The fruit is disposed with care in a glass vessel and is covered with brandy in which the fruit has been macerated, after having added 125 to 150 grm. of sugar per liter. Brandied fruits require to have the sugar added as a measure of precaution to preserve their firmness and their color. The jars are hermetically sealed and exposed to a moderate temperature and away from the light.

Apricots.
Abricots.

The apricot (*Prunus armeniaca*, L.) was originally a native of the Orient and was introduced into Europe by the Romans in the time of Pliny. There are a number of varieties of the apricot. Some which are grown on trellises produce the earliest fruit as well as fruit remarkable for its size, but those which are used by the liquor manufacturer are less regular in form and color, but have a more agreeable taste. Apricots which have a fine odor should be chosen, and they are prepared for consumption in the following manner: Take apricots of a clear yellow, without being entirely ripe, beat with a cloth to remove the down, and pierce. Detach or loosen the stone from the fruit without removing it. Puncture the place where the stem was removed with a needle and throw into very cold water. Heat the water to 95° in a bright copper basin to whiten them. Remove from the fire for fifteen minutes, then heat anew until the fruit rises to the surface, when it is removed gently with a skimmer and put in a bucket containing very cold water. When the apricots are whitened and cold they are strained and placed on a sieve, and after draining are placed in a vessel containing white brandy at 56°. After six days of maceration the apricots can be sweetened and then they are placed in glass jars or vessels filled with a liquid composed of

Essence of apricot kernels . ....0·2 l.
Alcohol (85°)................ 2   l. 800 c. c.
Sugar........................... .2   k. 500 grm.
Water.... 5   l. 300 c. c.

Product, 10 l. of fine fruit juice.

To obtain the ordinary juice of fruits the following should be used:

Essence of apricot kernels ....0·2 l.
Alcohol (85°) 2   l. 400 c. c.
Sugar... 1   k. 275 grm.
Water.......................... .6   l. 500 c. c.

Pineapple.

The pineapple (*Ananassa vulgaris*, L.) is a fruit of the tropics, but can also be cultivated in hothouses. This forced culture has reached great development in

France, Belgium, Holland and England. India, South America and the warm parts of North America and Oceanica consume vast quantities of pineapples and the fruit has acquired great commercial importance. Factories for preserving pineapples are in operation in India, Singapore, the Antilles, particularly in Martinique.

The Appert system is largely used. In the French colonies M. De Lavesan has successfully cultivated a number of varieties, including the common, pineapples without prickles, a pyramidal variety and a kind which produces mammoth fruit. The pulp of the pineapple and its juice produces a strong alcoholic liquor, which is largely consumed in warm countries. On the Congo a brandy is extracted from which a very pleasant liquor is prepared.

Brandied pineapple is prepared the same as oranges, lemons or angelica. The fruit is either left entire or cut in pieces.

Angelica.
Angélique.

Brandied angelica is prepared from the beautiful glassy stem, which is cut in pieces three or four inches long. Its further treatment is the same as for oranges.

Citron.
Cédrat.

The citron (*Citrus medici*) is a fruit of an ovoid form, with a thick skin, the color being a clear yellow. The peel of the citron contains a volatile oil of a yellow color, somewhat resembling that of the lemon. The skin of the citron being thicker than that of the lemon, it is employed in preference to the lemon for making the preserved peel. The principal countries which produce the citron are the tropical countries, India, Antilles and in some of the isles of Oceanica. In Europe in Provence, Spain, Italy, Malta, Africa, Algeria. Brandied citron is prepared in the same manner as brandied oranges, figs, etc.

Cherries.
Cérises.

Like the majority of the fruits already mentioned, the cherry is a native of Asia. It was imported into Italy by Lucullus. There are a number of varieties of cherries, which grow extensively in France, Hungary, etc. Cherries which are to be preserved in brandy must be large, fresh, and without spots or bruises. The stem is cut to half its length. The cherries are thrown in cold water to harden and to wash them. They are then strained and put in a cellar in a vessel containing alcohol prepared in the following manner:

Essence of coriander....	250 c. c.
Essence of Chinese cinnamon... .	100 c. c.
Essence of cloves............. ··	50 c. c.
Alcohol (85°).....................	5 l. 800 c. c.
Water............	3 l. 800 c. c.

Product, 10 l. of alcohol at 53°.

After six days of maceration put the cherries in a vessel and cover with a juice prepared as follows:

Brandy prepared from cherries...	6 l.
Sugar...............	1 k. 250 grm.
Water....... ···	3 l. 100 c. c.

Product, 10 l.

For first quality juice take:

Cherry brandy......	6 l. 500 c. c.
Sugar........	2 k. 500 grm.
Water.... ··	1 l. 800 c. c.

Oranges.

The Seville orange or *chinois*, a bitter orange (*Citrus bigaradia*), is used principally for preserving green. The skin of the ripe orange is used in making curaçao.

The bitter orange is a native of all warm countries and can be grown also in a hothouse. It is this kind of orange which is generally used for ornament. The most highly esteemed fruit for this purpose comes from the island of Curaçao, which has given its name to the liquor made from them. A variety with a similar skin but much less highly perfumed is grown in Italy and the heart of France. The fruit used chiefly in France for preserving comes principally from Italy, Provence and Algeria.

Those which are chosen are of small size and when they are cleaned they are whitened in the following manner: The oranges are placed in a basin containing water, which is then boiled to soften them.

They are then thrown in fresh water and left to soak
three or four days, renewing the water several times
each day to draw off the bitterness of the fruit.   The
fruit is immersed seven times in a sirup marking 12°
and augmented each time by four degrees.

The oranges are then thrown into a liquor prepared
as follows :

Alcohol (85°)...................	3 l. 200 c. c.
Sugar.	875 grm.
Water........................	5 l. 500 c. c.

For 10 l.

It is often advantageous to use preserved fruits.   In
this case treat the oranges as follows : Take the preserved fruit, put it on the fire with a small quantity of
water.   When the sugar is dissolved out, the fruit is
allowed to cool in the same water and then it is placed
in a vessel with the liquor named above.

Chestnuts.
Marrons.

The common chestnut (*Casteana vulgaris,* L.) grows
in Europe, Asia Minor, America, as well as in Asia,
where it originated.   It is a large tree, furnishing a
good quality of wood, and the nuts have a considerable
commercial value.   It grows by preference in a sandy
soil, in granitic soil, in ferruginous, slaty soil or in
silicious-argillaceous soil.

When it is desired to put chestnuts in brandy, preserved chestnuts must be used.   Take chestnuts preserved in sugar and put them in a basin with enough
water to wash them, warm the basin to assist the
water in dissolving the sugary envelope, then allow
the water to cool.   The chestnuts are then placed in a
liquid composed as follows :

Alcohol (85°)......................	3 l.
Sugar....	1 k. 375 grm.

Raise the volume to 10 l. by adding water in which
the chestnuts were soaked to remove the sugar.

Walnuts.
Noix.

The walnut is the fruit of the walnut tree (*Juglans
regia,* L.), originally a tree of Persia.   There are a number of varieties of the walnut which differ in size or

form.   Walnuts preserved in brandy are prepared in the same manner as chestnuts, the sugared fruit being washed to remove the sugar.

Peaches.
Pêches.

The peach (*Amygdalus persica*, L.) is, like the apricot, a native of Asia.   It was brought into Europe in the time of the Emperor Claudius.   Pliny was the first to give an exact description.   He assures us that it came from Persia to Italy by way of Egypt and Rhodes.   The peach is cultivated on trees and occasionally on trellises.   The preparation of brandied peaches is as follows : Select fine peaches just before they reach maturity, prepare them in the same manner as for apricots, then cover them with white brandy at 58°.   The juice can also be used to sweeten the peaches and other fruits having a pit.

Pears.
Poires.

The pear (*Pyrus*, L.) grows spontaneously in the forests of temperate Europe.   The Romans carried it from Gaul to Italy.   This tree is largely cultivated in France.

The pears are picked a little green, they are then stabbed to the center and whitened in water at 95°. When they begin to soften they are thrown in cold water.   After cooling, the fruit is peeled and placed in cold water acidulated with lemon juice, then, after draining, is placed in brandy at 53°

Plums.
Prunes.

The plum (*Prunus domestica*) is a fruit tree which depends little upon the kind of soil in which it is grown.   There are a number of varieties of the plum. The different kinds have little interest for American manufacturers.   The following is a description of the process of preserving one kind, and this will answer for all.   Choose well formed plums, without blemish and very green, cut off the end of the stem, pierce to the center and place in cold water to harden.   Then heat water to 95° in a bright red copper basin and add a little sea salt.   Throw the plums in this water and leave the fruit until it rises to the top, and put them in cold water several times to refresh them, during an hour or two. The plums are then drained and recovered with white wine at 53° or 56°.

Grapes.
Raisins.

The variety chosen is generally the Muscatel. Grapes are preserved in the following manner : The grapes are chosen before they are perfectly ripe. The large grapes are taken one at a time and passed through water and pricked. The smaller grapes are crushed and the juice is mixed with three times its weight of brandy at 56°. This having been done, the smaller grapes are pressed and the juice is mixed with three and one-half times its weight of brandy at 56°, after 250 to 300 grm. of sugar per liter has been dissolved in it. This juice is filtered and serves to cover the choice grapes.

CHAPTER II.

Fruit Preserves.

Apricots.

CHOOSE large, fine apricots of a good color, whiten them as already directed for brandied apricots. Wash them in fresh water and drain on a sieve, or more properly, on a napkin. Arrange the fruit in the jar so as to make it hold the largest number of pieces without crowding. Fill the jars with white cold sirup at 26°. Fasten the cover, or wire down, put in a water bath and boil for three minutes.

Pineapples.

Cut off the ends and pare the pineapple, cut in slices, fill the bottles or jars to about two-thirds their capacity, then fill with cold white sirup at 15°. Fasten on the covers tightly, heat to 100° C. in a water bath for one-half hour.

Cherries.

Use fine cherries, not too ripe, without spots or bruised pieces. Cut off the stems so as to leave only about 1 centimeter (one third inch). Fill the bottles with the fruit, using great care, and cover with cold white sirup at 24°. After bottling, cork tightly, put on a water bath and boil for twenty minutes.

Strawberries.

The strawberry (*Fragaria vesca*, L.) is an indigenous plant growing wild in the woods. There are numerous varieties which are obtained by cultivation.

.   .   .   .   .   .

Strawberry preserve is made as follows : Take the good fruit ripe and gather in dry weather. After having been hulled, they are placed in bottles which are filled with a cold sirup of 28°. After bottling, cork, wire down and carry the bottles to the boiling point and allow them to boil for some minutes over a water bath.

Raspberries.

The raspberry (*Rubis idens*, L.) like the strawberry, grows spontaneously in forests. The raspberry is exceedingly delicate and requires great care in preserving, which is done in the following manner : Take the fruit before it is completely ripe, hull and pack in bottles or jars so as not to crowd, but still fill the jar to its greatest capacity. Fill with cold sirup at 26°. Boil for some minutes on a water bath.

Currants.

The currant (*Ribes*, L.) comprises three kinds :
1. The red currant (*Ribes rubrum*, L.)
2. The prickly currant (*Ribes uva-crispa*, L.)
3. The black currant (*Ribes nigrum*, L.)
The first two grow naturally in the woods and hedges, but their fruit possesses no perfume.

Currants are preserved in the following manner : Take fine red or white currants, remove from the bunch and place in bottles. Then add the cold sirup at 36° and boil once.

Chestnuts.

Take fine chestnuts which have been treated three times with sugar and fill the bottles and add cold sirup at 32° and boil for three minutes.

Walnuts.

Walnuts are prepared in the same manner as chestnuts, only they are boiled five minutes.

Peaches.

Peaches are prepared in the same manner as apricots.

Pears.

Whiten the pears and drain. Give them four baths in the sugar and fill with a cold sirup of 28° and boil for eight minutes.

Plums.

The first step in the process is the same as for brandied plums. When the plums are whitened, cooled and drained they are placed in bottles with sirup of 28°. Cork, wire, and boil for five minutes.

CHAPTER III.

PRESERVATION OF FRUITS BY THE APPERT PROCESS.

THE principle of the Appert process of preserving fruits is based on the destruction by heat of the ferments and the germs which are inclosed in them. This process might also be called sterilizing fruits.

The process is worked as follows :

1. Shut up the bottles or other vessels with the fruit in them.

2. Seal the bottles up tightly.

3. Submit the bottles to the action of boiling water in the water bath for a length of time depending on the substance.

The success of the operation depends in a great measure on the following :

1. In the choice of bottles, which must be in good condition.

2. The finest corks should be used.

3. They must be corked with the greatest care, the cork being fastened with wire or in the same manner as champagne bottles.

4. The bottles or jars are enveloped in linen or placed in bags made expressly for the purpose.

5. The vessel in which they are placed is filled with water and maintained at 60° without boiling, to prevent evaporation, which would require a new supply to be added.

6. It is better to draw off the water than to remove the bottles to cool them.

7. The bottles are then sealed with wax and may then be put in a place where they will be exposed to the air.

An important improvement in the Appert process was introduced in 1839. The jars are placed in the water bath and are covered with a metallic cover in which a small hole is punched. This small aperture allows the last traces of air as well as vapor to escape. A drop of solder closes the orifice.

If the operation has been well conducted, the metal cover should be slightly bulged out, even if the small hole is left, but a no less dispensable condition is that this convexity must disappear on cooling and a pronounced concavity should take its place. If this does not happen, use the contents immediately. This convexity, as will be readily understood, is due to the internal pressure produced by the vapor of water and the trace of air which remains. When cooling takes place, these vapors are condensed and the interior becomes less than the exterior, hence the concavity. If the convexity continue, it is certain that the internal pressure is produced by some other substance besides the vapor of water.

When after several days, or even sometimes months, the top is swelled up to any great extent the phenomenon is the sign of a deep alteration in the preserves, which have been improperly sterilized, or, in other words, the fruit ferments. M. Gannal has given a sure means of guaranteeing the product. It is to maintain a moderate temperature in a stove for a month after preserving. If the swelling of the top does not occur, it is very certain it will not do so. The general method having been given, it will be necessary to indicate the modifications in the process which the various fruits make necessary.

Preserved Apricots.

Ripe fruit is preferred, but still only fruit should be chosen which offers a certain resistance. The pit is removed as well as the skin, which allows some chance for fermentation. The apricots are introduced in bottles provided with large mouths, so as to hold as many as possible without crowding. Cork tightly and place in the water bath. After boiling once, allow the bottles to cool. Then place the bottles in a cool place.

Pineapple Preserves.

For a number of years the manufacture of pineapple preserve has obtained considerable development in the countries where the fruit is grown. As it is difficult to obtain bottles of the right shape to preserve an entire pineapple, as well as the trouble in transporting, tin cans are extensively used. Pineapples, owing to relative volume, must be heated for a long time.

Cherry Preserves.

Cherries are introduced entire in glass vessels and piled up gently. They are heated for a few minutes, but much less than apricots.

Raspberry Preserves.

Raspberries are preserved in the same manner as currants, but it is a very difficult operation, which must be conducted with care to obtain the best results.

Currant Preserves.

Currants may be preserved by the Appert process for a year or more, but if the aroma and the odor remain intact, the same is not true of the form, which is sacrificed if extraordinary precautions are not taken. Currants, after having been separated from the stem, are introduced in bottles so as to leave as little air space as possible. Cork tightly and heat on a water bath, as has been already described.

Peach Preserves.

It is very difficult to preserve peaches so as to preserve their form, this fruit being very delicate. The variety of peach is chosen which has the most aroma. They are preserved at their maturity without being too ripe. They are cut in two to remove the stone and are in turn redivided if necessary. They are piled as tightly as possible, some almonds are added and the bottle is tightly corked and put on a water bath, and is put in bottles and given one or two boilings. Remove the fire from the water bath and allow it to cool. When the water is cold remove the bottles and put in a place which has a good circulation of air, but not too damp.

Other fruits are preserved in this general manner, the time of heating depending upon the size of the fruit and the difficulty or ease with which it can be sterilized.

PART IV.—ANALYSIS AND ADULTERATIONS.

CHAPTER I.

ANALYSIS OF ALCOHOLS AND LIQUORS.

SECTION I.—ALCOHOL.

IN pure alcohol two elements must be determined:

1.—The quantity of absolute alcohol contained in the liquid, that is to say, the alcoholic degree.

2.—The purity of the product, that is to say, if the alcohol is only a mixture of ethyl alcohol and water, or if it contains aldehyde and the superior alcohols—amylic, propylic, butyric, etc.

Determination of the Alcoholic Strength. —This operation is very simple and is made by means of the centesimal alcoholometer of Gay-Lussac (Fig. 56), the use of which has become obligatory in France by the law of July 8, 1881, put in effect by the decree of December 27, 1884. It is a densimeter of constant weight, graduated so as to obtain the richness in alcohol of mixtures of alcohol and water, provided it contains no other material. The alcohol to be tested is placed in a high jar, the alcoholometer is placed in it, and when equilibrium has been attained the graduation corresponding to the lowest part of the meniscus is read.

At the same time the temperature of the liquid is determined by means of a thermometer, so that the correction for temperature may be made, the alcoholometers being graduated at a temperature of 15° C., and a correction must be made for all other temperatures. To facilitate or rather eliminate this correction Gay-Lussac's tables are used. The tables are constructed as follows: On the first horizontal line is given the apparent

FIG. 56.

strength, that is to say, the degree marked by the alcoholometer when it is plunged in the liquid at the temperature of the surroundings. In the first vertical column are inscribed all temperatures between 0° and 30° (Centigrade). The real strength of the liquid will be found at the point of intersection of the vertical column, which is commenced by the apparent strength, and the horizontal line, which corresponds to the actual temperature. The volume, which at 15° (C.) would occupy 1,000 liters measured at the temperature at which the apparent strength has been taken, is given by the number inscribed under the figures representing the actual strength, or, if there is none, by the first number encountered at the left on the same line.

GAY-LUSSAC'S TABLES.

TABLE I.

INDICATIONS OF THE ALCOHOLOMETER.

APPARENT STRENGTH.

Temperatures	1°	2°	3°	4°	5°	6°	7°	8°	9°	10°	11°	12°	13°	14°	15°	16°	17°	18°	19°	20°
0°	1.3 1000	2.4	3.4	4.4	5.4	6.5 1001	7.5	8.6	9.7	10.9	12.2	13.4 1002	14.7	16.1	17.5	18.9 1003	20.3	21.6 1004	22.9	24.2
1												13.4 1002	14.7	16	17.3	18.7 1003	20	21.3 1004	22.6 1004	23.9
2												13.4 1002	14.7	16	17.2	18.5 1003	19.8	21.1	22.3 1004	23.6
3												13.4 1002	14.6	15.9	17.1	18.3 1003	19.6	20.8	22	23.3 1004
4												13.3 1001	14.5 1002	15.8	16.9	18.1 1003	19.4	20.6	21.8	23
5	1.4 1001	2.5	3.5	4.5	5.5	6.6	7.7	8.7	9.8	10.9	12.1	13.3 1001	14.4	15.7 1002	16.8	18	19.2	20.4 1003	21.5	22.7
6												13.1 1001	14.3	15.6 1002	16.7	17.8	19	20.2 1003	21.3	22.4
7												13 1001	14.2	15.4 1002	16.6 1002	17.7	18.8 1002	20	21	22.1
8												13 1001	14.1	15.3	16.4	17.5	18.6 1002	19.7	20.7	21.8
9	1.4 1001	2.4	3.5	4.5	5.5	6.5	7.5	8.5	9.5	10.6	11.7	12.9 1001	14	15.1	16.2	17.3	18.4	19.5	20.5 1002	21.6
10	1.4 1001	2.4	3.4 1001	4.4	5.5	6.5	7.5	8.5	9.5	10.6	11.7	12.7	13.8	14.9	16	17	18.1	19.2	20.2 1002	21.3
11	1.3 1000	2.4	3.4	4.4 1:01	5.4	6.4	7.4	8.4	9.4	10.5	11.6	12.6	13.6	14.7	15.8	16.8	17.9	19	20	21
12	1.2 1000	2.3	3.3	4.3	5.3	6.3	7.3	8.3	9.3	10.4	11.5 1001	12.5 1001	13.5	14.6	15.6	16.6	17.6	18.7	19.7	20.7

13	4.2 / 1000	5.2	6.2	7.2	8.2	9.2	10.3	11.4	12.4	13.4	14.4	15.4	16.4	17.4	18.5	19.5	20.5
14	1.1 / 1000	5.1	6.1	7.1	8.1	9.1	10.2	11.2	12.2	13.2	14.2	15.2	16.2	17.2	18.2	19.2	20.2
15	1 / 1000	5	6	7	8	9	10	11	12	13	14	15	16	17	18	19	20
16	0.9 / 1000	4.9	5.9	6.9	7.9	8.9	9.9	10.9	11.9	12.9	13.9	14.9	15.9	16.9	17.9	18.7	19.7
17	0.8 / 1000	4.8	5.8	6.8	7.8	8.8	9.8	10.8	11.7	12.7	13.7	14.7	15.6	16.6	17.5	18.4	19.4
18	0.7 / 1000	4.7	5.7	6.7	7.7	8.7	9.7	10.7	11.6	12.5 / 990	13.5	14.5	15.4	16.3	17.3	18.2 / 999	19.1
19	0.6 / 999	4.5	5.5	6.5	7.5	8.5	9.5	10.5	11.4	12.4	13.3	14.3	15.2	16.1	17	17.9	18.8
20	0.4 / 999	4.4	5.4	6.4	7.3	8.3	9.3	10.3	11.2	12.2	13.1	14	14.9	15.8	16.7	17.6	18.5
21	0.3 / 999	4.3	5.2	6.2	7.1	8.1	9.1	10.1	11	11.9	12.8	13.7	14.6	15.5	16.4	17.3	18.2
22	0.1 / 999	4.1	5.1	6.1	7	8	8.9	9.9 / 997	10.8	11.7	12.6 / 998	13.5	14.4	15.3	16.2	17	17.9
23	1 / 999	4	5	5.9	6.8 / 998	7.8	8.7	9.7	10.6 / 998	11.5	12.4	13.3	14.1	15	15.9	16.7 / 998	17.6
24	0.8 / 998	3.8	4.8	5.8	6.7	7.6	8.5	9.5	10.4	11.3	12.2	13.1	13.9	14.8	15.7 / 997	16.5	17.4
25	0.8 / 998	3.6	4.6	5.4	6.5	7.4	8.4	9.3	10.2 / 997	11.1	12 / 997	12.9	13.8	14.5 / 997	15.4	16.2	17.1
26	0.7 / 998	3.5	4.4	5	6.3	7.2	8.1	9	9.9	10.8	11.7	12.6	13.4	14.2	15.1	15.9	16.8
27	0.5 / 998	3.4	4.3	4.8	6.1	7	7.9	8.8 / 997	9.7	10.6	11.5	12.3	13.1	14	14.8	15.6	16.5
28	0.5 / 998	3.3	4.1	4.6	5.9	6.8	7.7	8.6	9.5	10.3	11.2	12	12.8 / 996	13.6 / 996	14.5	15.3	16.1
29	0.4 / 997	3.1	3.9	4.8	5.7	6.6	7.5	8.4	9.2	10.1	11	11.8	12.6	13.4	14.2	15	15.8
30	0.9 / 997	2.8	3.7	4.6	5.5	6.4	7.3	8.1	9 / 996	9.8	10.7	11.5	12.3	13.3	13.9	14.7	15.5

TABLE II.

INDICATIONS OF THE ALCOHOLOMETER.

APPARENT STRENGTH.

Températures:	21°	22°	23°	24°	25°	26°	27°	28°	29°	30°	31°	32°	33°	34°	35°	36°	37°	38°	39°	40°
0°	25.6 / 1005	27	28.4 / 1006	29.7 / 1006	30.9 / 1007	32.1	33.2	34.3 / 1008	35.3	36.3	37.3 / 1009	38.3	39.2	40.2	41.1	42.1 / 1010	43.1	44	45	45.9
1	25.3 / 1005	26.7	28	29.2 / 1006	30.4 / 1006	31.6	32.7 / 1007	33.8	34.8	35.8 / 1008	36.8	37.8	38.8	39.8	40.8 / 1009	41.8	42.7	43.7	44.6 / 1010	45.5
2	25.3 / 1005	26.3	27.5	28.8 / 1006	30 / 1006	31.2	32.3 / 1007	33.3	34.4 / 1007	35.4	36.4	37.4	38.4 / 1008	39.4	40.4	41.4	42.3	43.3 / 1009	44.2	45.1
3	24.9 / 1004	25.9 / 1005	27.1 / 1005	28.4	29.6 / 1006	30.8 / 1006	31.9	32.9	33.9 / 1007	34.9	36	37	38 / 1008	39	40	41 / 1008	42	43.3 / 1009	43.9	44.8
4	24.6 / 1001	25.6 / 1005	26.8 / 1005	28	29.2	30.8 / 1006	31.4	32.5	33.5 / 1007	34.5	35.5	36.5	37.5	38.5 / 1007	39.5	40.5	41.5	42.5	43.5	44.8 / 1008
5	24 / 1003	25.2	26.4 / 1004	27.6	28.8 / 1005	30	31 / 1005	32.1	33.1 / 1006	34.1	35.1	36.1 / 1006	37.1 / 1007	38.1	39.1	40.1	41.1 / 1007	42.1	43.1	44.4
6	23.6 / 1003	24.9	26 / 1004	27.2 / 1004	28.4	29.6 / 1005	30.6 / 1005	31.6	32.6 / 1006	33.6	34.7	35.7 / 1006	36.7	37.7	38.7	39.7 / 1006	40.7 / 1007	41.6	42.6	43.6
7	23.3 / 1003	24.6 / 1003	25.7 / 1004	26.9	28	29.2	30.2 / 1004	31.2	32	33.2	34.2	35.2	36.2	37.2 / 1005	38.2	39.2 / 1006	40.2	41.2	42.2	43.2
8	23 / 1002	24.2	25.3 / 1003	26.5	27.6	28.8	29.8 / 1004	30.8	31.8	32.8	33.8 / 1004	34.8	35.8 / 1004	36.8	37.8	38.8	39.8	40.8 / 1005	41.8	42.8 / 1005
9	22.7 / 1002	23.9	25	26.1	27.2 / 1003	28.4	29.4 / 1003	30.4	31.4	32.4 / 1004	33.4 / 1004	34.4	35.4	36.4	37.4 / 1004	38.4	39.4	40.4	41.4	42.4
10	22.4 / 1001	23.5 / 1002	24.6 / 1001	25.7	26.8 / 1003	28.4 / 1003	29	30	31	32	33	34	35 / 1003	36	37 / 1004	38	39	40	41	42
11	22.1 / 1001	23.2	24.3	25.4	26.5 / 1002	27.6	28.6	29.6	30.6	31.6	32.6	33.6 / 1003	34.6	35.6	36.6	37.6	38.6	39.6	40.6 / 1003	41.6
12	21.8 / 1001	22.9	24	25.1	26.1	27.2	28.2	29.2	30.2	31.2	32.2	33.2	34.2 / 1002	35.2	36.2	37.2	38.2	39.2	40.2 / 1003	41.2

	21.5	22.6	22.3	23.6	24.7	25.7	26.8	27.8	28.8	29.8	30.8	31.8	32.8	33.8	34.8	35.8	36.8	37.8	38.8	39.8	40.8
13	21.5	22.6	22.3	23.6	24.7	25.7	26.8	27.8	28.8	29.8	30.8	31.8	32.8	33.8	34.8	35.8	36.8	37.8	38.8	39.8	40.8
14	21.2	22.3	23.3	24.3	25.3	26.4	27.4	28.4	29.4	30.4	31.4	32.4	33.4	34.4	35.4	36.4	37.4	38.4	39.4	40.4	
15	21	22	23	24	25	26	27	28	29	30	31	32	33	34	35	36	37	38	39	40	
16	20.7	21.7	22.7	23.7	24.7	25.7	26.6	27.6	28.6	29.6	30.6	31.6	32.5	33.5	34.5	35.5	36.4	37.4	38.4	39.5	
17	20.4	21.4	22.4	23.4	24.4	25.4	26.3	27.3	28.2	29.2	30.2	31.2	32.1	33	34	34.1	35.1	37.1	38	39.1	
18	20.1	21.1	22	23	24	25	25.9	26.9	27.6	28.8	29.8	30.8	31.7	32.7	33.7	34.7	35.7	36.7	37	38.7	
19	19.8	20.8	21.7	22.7	23.6	24	25.5	26.5	27.4	27.6	28.6	30.4	31.3	34.1	33.3	33.3	34.3	36.3	37	38.3	
20	19.5	20.5	21.4	22.4	23.3	24.3	25.2	26.1	27.1	27.4	28	30.4	31	32	33.3	32.9	33.9	35.9	36.3	37.9	
21	19.1	20.1	21.1	22.1	23	23.9	26.1	25.2	28	27.6	29	30	30.9	30.5	32.5	32.5	33.5	35.3	36.5	37.5	
22	18.8	19.8	20.7	21.7	22.6	23.6	25.3	25.7	26.3	27.6	28.6	30	29.7	31.5	32.1	33.1	33.1	35.1	36.1	37.1	
23	18.5	19.5	20.4	21.4	22.3	23.2	25	24.6	25.9	26.8	27.8	28	29.7	31.7	32	31.3	32.7	34.7	35.7	36.7	
24	18.3	19.2	20.1	21.1	21.9	22.8	24.1	24.6	25.5	26.4	27.4	28	29.3	30.3	30.3	31.3	33	34.3	35	36.3	
25	18	18.9	19.8	20.7	21.6	22.5	23.3	24.3	25.2	26.1	27	28	29	29	30.9	30.5	31.9	33.9	34	35.9	
26	17.7	18.6	19.5	20.4	21.3	22.2	23	23.9	24.8	25.7	26.6	27.6	28	29.5	29.5	30.5	31.5	33.5	34.5	35.5	
27	17.4	18.3	19.2	20.1	20.9	21.8	22.7	23.6	24.4	25.3	26.2	28.2	27.2	28.3	30.1	30.1	31.1	33.1	34.1	35.1	
28	17	18	18.9	19.7	20.6	21.5	22.3	23.2	24	24.9	25.8	26.8	27.7	28.7	29.7	30.7	31.7	32.7	33	34.7	
29	16.7	17.6	18.5	19.4	20.3	21.1	21.9	22.8	23.7	24.5	25.4	26.4	26.4	28.3	28.3	29.3	30.3	32.3	33.3	34.3	
30	16.4	17.3	18.2	19.1	19.9	20.8	21.6	22.5	23.3	24.2	25	26	27	27.9	27.9	28.9	29.9	30.9	31.9	32.9	33.9

TABLE III.

INDICATIONS OF THE ALCOHOLOMETER.

APPARENT STRENGTH.

Temperatures	41°	42°	43°	44°	45°	46°	47°	48°	49°	50°	51°	52°	53°	54°	55°	56°	57°	58°	59°	60°
0	46.9 (1011)	47.9	48.8	49.8	50.7	51.7 (1012)	52.6 (1012)	53.5	54.5	55.4	56.4	57.3	58.3	59.2	60.2	61.2	62.4 (1013)	63.1 (1013)	63.8	64.1
1	46.5 (1010)	47.5	48.4	49.4	50.3	51.3 (1011)	52.2 (1011)	53.2	54.2	55.1	56	57	57.9	58	59.9	60.9	61.8	62.8 (1012)	63.8	64.7
2	46.1 (1009)	47.1	48.1	49	49.9 (1010)	50.9	51.8	52.8	53.8	54.7	55.7	56.6	57.6	58.5	59.5	60.5	61.5	62.4	63.4	64.4
3	46.1 (1009)	46.7 (1009)	47.7	48.6	49.6	50.5	51.5	52.4	53.4	54.3	55.3	56.3	57.2	58.5	59.2	60.2 (1011)	61.4	62.4	63.1	64.1
4	45.8 (1008)	46.4 (1009)	47.4	48.3	49.3	50.2	51.1	52.1	53	54 (1009)	54.3	55.2	56.2	57.8 (1010)	58.9	59.2	60.4	61.7	62.7	63.7
5	45.4 (1008)	45.9	46.9	47.9	48.8	49.8	50.7 (1008)	51.7	52.7	53.6	54.3	55.2	56.2	57.1	58.5	59.5	60.1 (1008)	61	62.4	63
6	45 (1007)	45.5 (1006)	46.5 (1007)	47.5 (1007)	48.4	49.4	50.4	51.4	52.4	53.3	54.3	54.9	55.9	36.8	57.8	58.8	59.8 (1007)	60.7 (1008)	61.7	62.7
7	44.6 (1006)	45.1	46.1	47.1	48.1	49.1	50.1	51	52	52.9	53.9	54.9	55.9	36.5	57.5	58.5	59.5	60.4	61.4	62.4
8	44.2 (1005)	44.8 (1006)	45	46	47.7	48.7	49.7	50.6	51.6	52.6 (1006)	53.6	54.6	55.5	36.5	57.5	58.5	59	60	61	62
9	43.8 (1005)	44.4	45	46	47.3	48.3	49.3 (1005)	50.6	51.4	52.4	53.2	54.2	55.1	36.1	57.1	58.1	59	60	61	62
10	43.4 (1004)	44 (1004)	44.6	46	46.9	47.9	48.9	49.9	50.9	51.9	52.9	53.8	54	35	56.8	57.8	58.8	59.7	60.7	61.7
11	43 (1004)	43.6 (1004)	44.4	45.6	46.6	47.6	48.6	49.5	50.5	51.5	53.5	53.5	54.4	35.4	56.4	57.4	58.4	59.4	60.4	61.4
12	42.6 (1003) 42.2 (1002)	43.2 (1003)	44.2	45.2	46.2	47.2	48.2	49.2	50.2	51.1	52.1	53.1	54.1	55	56	57	58	59	60	61

	43	44	45	46	47	48	49	50	51	52	53	54	55	56	57	58	59	60	60
	42.8	43.8	44.8	45.8	46.8	47.8	48.9	49.9	50.8	51.8	52.7	53.7	54.7	55.7	56.7	57.7	58.7	59.7	60.7
13	42.8	43.8	44.8	45.8	46.8	47.8	48.9	49.9	50.8	51.8	52.7	53.7	54.7	55.7	56.7	57.7	58.7	59.7	60.7
14 (1001)	42.4	43.4	44.4	45.4	46.4	47.4	48.4	49.4	50.4	51.4	52.3	53.3	54.3	55.3	56.3	57.3	58.3	59.3	60.9
15 (1000)	41.4			3.9				50		52		54		56	57	58	59	60	60
16 (1000)	40.6	42.6	43.6	44.0	45.0	46.6	47.6	48.6	49.6	50.6	51.6	52.6	53.6	54	55.6	56.6	57.6	58.6	59.6
17 (999)	40.2	42.2	3.9	44.2	45.2	46.2	47.2	48.3	49.3	50.3	51.3	52.3	53.3	54.3	55.3	56.3	57.3	58.3	59
18 (998)	39.8	41.8	42.8	43.8	44.9	45.9	46.9	47.9	48.9	49.9	50.9	51.9	52.9	53.9	54.9	55.9	56.9	57.9	58.9
19 (997)	39.4	40.4	41.4	42.5	43.5	44.5	45.5	46.5	47.5	48.5	49.5	50.6	51.6	52.6	53.6	54.6	55.6	56.6	57.6 (997)
20 (997)	39	40	42	42.1	43.1	44.1	45.1	46.1	47.2	48.2	49.2	50.2	51.2	52.2	53.2	54.2	55.2	56.2	57.2
21 (196)	38.6	39.6	40.6	41.7	42.7	43.7	44.8	45.8	46.8	47.8	48.8	49.8	50.8	51.8	52.9	53.9	54.9	55.9	56.9
22 (996)	38.2	39.2	40.2	41.3	42.3	43.3	44.3	45.3	46.4	47.4	48.4	49.4	50.4	51.4	52.5	53.5	54.5	55.5	56.5
23 (995)	37.8	38.8	39.8	40.9	41.9	42.9	43.9	44.9	46	47	48	49.1	50.1	51.1	52.1	53.1	54.1	55.1	56.1
24 (995)	37.4	38.4	39.4	40.5	41.5	42.5	43.6	44.6	45.6	46.6	47.6	48.7	49.7	50.7	51.8	52.8	53.8	54.8	55.8 (992)
25 (994)	37	38	39	40.1	41.1	42.1	43.2	44.2	45.2	46.3	47.3	48.3	49.3	50.3	51.4	52.4	53.4	54.5	55.5
26 (994)	36.5	37.6	38.6	39.7	40.7	41.8	42.8	43.8	44.9	45.9	46.9	47.9	49	50	51	52	53	54	55.1
27 (993)	36.1	37.2	38.2	39.3	40.3	41.4	42.4	43.4	44.5	45.5	46.5	47.6	48.6	49.6	50.7	51.7	52.7	53.7	54.8
28 (992)	35.7	36.7	37.8	38.9	39.9	41	42	43	44.1	45.1	46.1	47.2	48.2	49.2	50.3	51.3	52.3	53.3	54.4 (989)
29 (991)	35.3	36.3	37.4	38.5	39.5	40.6	41.6	42.6	43.7	44.7	45.7	46.8	47.8	48.9	49.9	51	52	53	54
30 (991)	34.9	35.9	37	38.1	39.1	40.2	41.2	42.3	43.3	44.3	45.4	46.4	47.5	48.5	49.6	50.6	51.6	52.6	53.6 (988)

TABLE IV.

INDICATIONS OF THE ALCOHOLOMETER.

APPARENT STRENGTH.

Temperatures	61°	62°	63°	64°	65°	66°	67°	68°	69°	70°	71°	72°	73°	74°	75°	76°	77°	78°	79°	80°
0°	66 1013	67	68	68.9	69.9	70.8	71.8	72.7	73 7 1014	74.7	75.6	76.6	77.6	678	79	80.5	81.5	82	83.3	84.3
1	65.7 1012	66.7	67.7	68.6	69.6	70.5	71.5	72 4	73 4	74.3	75.3	76.3	77	78.3	79 2	80.2	81 2	82	83.1	84
2	65.3 1011	66.3	67.3	68.3	69.3	70.2	71 2 1012	72 1	73 1	74	75	76	77	78	78.9	79.9	80.9	81	82.8	83 7
3	65 1010	66	67	68	68.9	69.9 1011	70 8	71.8	72 8	73 7	74 7	75.7 76	76	77.7	78.6	79.6	80 6	81 6	82.5	83.5
4	64.7 1009	65.7 66	66.6 1010	67.6 1010	68.6 69.5	69.5	70.5 71	71 2	72 5	73 4	74.4 75	75	77.3	77.3	78	79.6 80	80 6	81	82.2 83	83 2
5	64.3 1009	65.3 66	66 3	67.3 1010	68	69	70 2	71 2	72.2 73	73 1	74 1 75	75	76	77.3	78	79.3	80 3	81.3	82.2 83	83 2
6	64	65	66	67	68	68.9	69	70	71	72.8	73.8 74	74	75	76.7	77	78.7	79.7	80.7	81.9 82	82 9
7	63.7 1008	64.7 65	65 7	66.7 1007	67.6	68.6	69	70	71.5	72.5	73.5 74	74	75	76	77	78.4	79.7	80.7	81.9 1010	81.6 82.6 1009
8	63.4 1007	64.4 64.4	65.4	66.4	67 3	68 3	69 3	70.3	71.2	72.2	73.2 74	74.1	75.1	76	77	78.2	79.4	80	81.4	82.3 1008
9	63 1005	64	65	66	67	67.9	68.9 69	69.9	70.9 71	71.9 72	72 73	73	74	75.6	76	77.2	78.9 79	80	81.1	81 82 1008
10	62.7 1005 1004	63.7 61.7	64.7	65 7	66.7	67	68	69	70.6 70	71	72	73	74 8 1005	75	76.5	77	78.8 1006	79	80.8	81.5 80.5
11	62.4 1004	63.7 64.4	64.7	65.4	66.4	67	68 3	69.3 1004	70.3 71	71.3	72.3 73	73	74.2 1005	75 2	76 2	77.2	78.2 79	79	80 2	81.2 80.2
12	62 1003 1002	64	64	65	66	67	63 69 1003	69	71	71	72	72.9 73	73 9	74.9 75	75.9 76	76 9 77	77 9 78	78	79.9 80	80.9

		62	63	64	65	66	67	68	69	70	71	72	73	74	75	76	77	78	79	80
13	61.7	62.7	63.7	64.7	65.7	66.7	67.7	68.7	69.6	70.6	71.6	72.6	73.6	74.6	75.6	76.6	77.6	78.6	79.6	80.6
14	61.3	62.3	63.3	64.3	65.3	66.3	67.3	68.3	69.3	70.3	71.3	72.3	73.3	74.3	75.3	76.3	77.3	78.3	79.3	80.3
15	61	62	63	64	65	66	67	68	69	70	71	72	73	74	75	76	77	78	79	80
16	60.6	61.7	62.7	63.7	64.7	65.7	66.7	67.7	68.7	69.7	70.7	71.7	72.7	73.7	74.7	75.7	76.7	77.7	78.7	79.7
17	60.3	61.3	62.3	63.3	64.3	65.3	66.3	67.3	68.4	69.4	70.4	71.4	72.4	73.4	74.4	75.4	76.4	77.4	78.4	79.4
18	59.9	61	62	63	64	65	66	67	68.1	69.1	70.1	71.1	72.1	73.1	74.1	75.1	76.1	77.1	78.1	79.1
19	59.6	60.6	61.6	62.7	63.7	64.7	65.7	66.7	67.7	68.7	69.7	70.7	71.7	72.7	73.7	74.7	75.8	76.8	77.8	78.8
20	59.2	60.3	61.3	62.3	63.3	64.3	65.4	66.4	67.4	68.4	69.4	70.4	71.4	72.4	73.4	74.4	75.5	76.5	77.5	78.5
21	58.9	59.9	61	62	63	64	65	66	67	68.1	69.1	70.1	71.1	72.1	73.1	74.1	75.2	76.2	77.2	78.2
22	58.5	59.5	60.5	61.6	62.7	63.7	64.7	65.7	66.7	67.8	68.8	69.8	70.8	71.8	72.8	73.8	74.8	75.9	76.9	77.9
23	58.1	59.2	60.2	61.3	62.3	63.3	64.3	65.4	66.4	67.4	68.4	69.4	70.5	71.5	72.5	73.5	74.5	75.5	76.6	77.6
24	57.8	58.9	59.9	61	62	63	64	65	66	67.4	68.4	69.4	70.4	71.4	72.4	73.4	74.4	75.4	76.4	77.3
25	57.5	58.5	59.5	60.6	61.6	62.6	63.6	64.7	65.7	66.7	67.8	68.8	69.8	70.8	71.8	72.8	73.9	74.9	75.9	77
26	57.1	58.1	59.2	60.2	61.3	62.3	63.3	64.3	65.3	66.3	67.4	68.4	69.4	70.5	71.5	72.5	73.6	74.6	75.6	76.7
27	56.8	57.8	58.9	59.9	60.9	61.9	63	64	65	66	67.1	68.1	69.1	70.2	71.2	72.2	73.3	74.3	75.3	76.3
28	56.4	57.5	58.5	59.5	60.6	61.6	62.6	63.7	64.7	65.7	66.8	67.8	68.8	69.9	70.9	71.9	73	74	75	76
29	56	57.1	58.1	59.2	60.2	61.2	62.3	63.3	64.3	65.4	66.4	67.4	68.5	69.5	70.6	71.6	72.6	73.7	74.7	75.7
30	55.7	56.7	57.7	58.8	59.9	60.9	61.9	63	64	65	66.1	67.1	68.2	69.2	70.3	71.3	72.3	73.3	74.3	75.3

TABLE V.

INDICATIONS OF THE ALCOHOLOMETER.

APPARENT STRENGTH.

Temperatures	81°	82°	83°	84°	85°	86°	87°	88°	89°	90°	91°	92°	93°	94°	95°	96°	97°	98°	99°	100°
0°	85.2 / 1014	86.2	87.1	88	88.9	89.9 / 1015	90.9	91.8	92.6	93	94.5	95.3	96.3	97.1	98	98.8	99.7			
1	85 / 1014	85.9	86.9	87.8	88.7	89.6 / 1014	90.5	91.5	92.4	93.3	94.3	95.1	96	96.9	97.8	98.6	1010 / 99.5	99.9		
2	84.7 / 1013	85.6	86.6	87.5	88.5	89.4 / 1014	90.3	91.3	92.2	93.1	94	94.9	95.8	96.7	97.6	98.5	99.3 / 1014			
3	84.7 / 1012	85.4	86.3	87.3	88.2	89.2 / 1013	90.1	91	91.9	92.9	93.8	94.7	95.6	96.5	97.4	98.3	99.2			
4	84.4 / 1011	85.1	86.1	87	87.9	89.2 / 1012	89.8	90.8	91.7	92.7	93.6	94.5	95.4	96.3	97.2	98.4	99	99.9		
5	84.2 / 1011	85.1	85.8	86.7	87.7	88 / 689	89.6	90.5	91.5	92.4	93.4	94.3	95.2	96.1	97	97.9	98.8	99.7		
6	83.9 / 1010	84.8	85.5	86.5	87.4	88.4 / 1011	89.3	90.2	91.2	92.2	93.1	93.9	94.8	95.7	96.6	97.6	98.5	99.6		
7	83.3 / 1009	84.2	85.2	86.2	87.2	88.1	89.1	90	91	91.9	92.9	93.9	94.4	95.4	96.4	97.4	98.3	99.2		
8	83 / 1008	84	85	85.9	86.9	87.9	88.9	89.8	90.7	91.7	92.7	93.6	94.6	95.5	96.4	97.4	98.1	99.1		
9	82.7 / 1007	83.7	84.7	85.7	86.6	87.6	88.6	89.5	90.5	91.5	92.5	93.4	94.4	95.3	96.2	97	98	98.9	100	
10	82.4 / 1006	83.4	84.4	85.4	86.4	87.4	88.3	89.3	90.2	91.2	92.2	93.2	94.2	95.1	96	97	97.8	98.9	99.9	
11	82.2 / 1005	83.1	84.1	85.1	86.1	87.1	88	89	90	91	92	92.9	93.9	94.9	95.8	96.8	97.8	98.7	99.7	
12	81.9 / 1004	82.9	83.9	84.8	85.8	86.8	87.8	88.7	89.7	90.7	91.7	92.7	93.7	94.7	95.6	96.6	97.6	98.5	99.5	

	82	83	84	85	86	87	88	89	90	91	92	93	94	95	96	97	98	99	100
13	81.6	82.6	83.6	84.6	85.5	86.5	87.5	88.5	89.5	90.5	91.5	92.5	93.5	94.4	95.4	96.4	97.4	98.4	99.3
1002																			
14	81.3	82.3	83.3	84.3	85.3	86.3	87.3	88.2	89.2	90.2	91.2	92.2	93.2	94.2	95.2	96.2	97.2	98.2	99.2
1001																			
15	81	82	83	84	85	86	87	88	89	90	91	92	93	94	95	96	97	98	99
1000																			
16	80.7	81.7	82.7	83.7	84.7	85.7	86.7	87.7	88.7	89.7	90.8	91.8	92.8	93.8	94.8	95.8	96.8	97.8	98.8
999																			
17	80.4	81.4	82.4	83.4	84.4	85.4	86.4	87.4	88.4	89.5	90.5	91.5	92.6	93.6	94.6	95.6	96.6	97.6	98.7
998																			
18	80.1	81.1	82.1	83.1	84.1	85.2	86.2	87.2	88.2	89.2	90.2	91.3	92.3	93.3	94.3	95.3	96.4	97.4	98.5
997																			
19	79.8	80.8	81.9	82.9	83.9	84.9	85.9	86.9	87.9	88.9	90	91	92	93	94	95.2	96.2	97.3	98.3
996																			
20	79.5	80.5	81.6	82.6	83.6	84.6	85.6	86.6	87.7	88.7	89.7	90.8	91.8	92.9	93.9	95	96	97.1	98.1
995																			
21	79.2	80.2	81.3	82.3	83.3	84.3	85.3	86.4	87.4	88.4	89.5	90.5	91.5	92.6	93.7	94.7	95.8	96.9	99
993																			
22	78.9	79.9	81	82	83	84	85	86.1	87.1	88.2	89.2	90.2	91.3	92.4	93.4	94.5	95.5	96.7	97.7
991																			
23	78.6	79.6	80.7	81.7	82.7	83.8	84.8	85.8	86.8	87.9	88.9	90	91.1	92.1	93.2	94.3	95.4	96.5	97.5
992																			
24	78.3	79.3	80.4	81.4	82.4	83.5	84.5	85.5	86.5	87.6	88.7	89.8	90.8	91.9	93	94.1	95.2	96.2	98.4
991																			
25	78	79	80.1	81.1	82.1	83.2	84.2	85.2	86.3	87.3	88.4	89.5	90.6	91.6	92.7	93.8	94.9	96	98.2
990																			
26	77.7	78.7	79.8	80.8	81.8	82.9	83.9	85	86	87.1	88.2	89.2	90.3	91.4	92.5	93.6	94.7	95.7	98.1
991																			
27	77.4	78.4	79.5	80.5	81.5	82.6	83.6	84.7	85.7	86.8	87.9	89	90.1	91.1	92.2	93.4	94.5	95.6	97.9
989																			
28	77.1	78.1	79.2	80.2	81.2	82.3	83.3	84.3	85.4	86.5	87.6	88.7	89.8	90.9	92	93.1	94.3	95.4	97.7
988																			
29	76.7	77.8	78.9	79.9	80.9	82	83.1	84.1	85.2	86.2	87.3	88.4	89.5	90.6	91.7	92.9	94.1	95.2	97.5
987																			
30	76.4	77.5	78.6	79.6	80.6	81.7	82.7	83.8	84.9	86	87.1	88.2	89.3	90.4	91.5	92.7	93.8	95	97.3
986															985		985		984

In 85° (Gay-Lussac) alcohol the examination to see if the rectification has been properly carried on is conducted as follows: 1. Tasting gives very good results for this trial. But as this requires long experience, other methods must be used.

2. M. Savalle has devised the following process, which is one of the best. Monohydrated sulphuric acid is a good reagent for determining the degree of purity of alcohol. Sulphuric acid, which should be colorless, is boiled with an equal volume of pure alcohol. Very little coloration will be observed, while the less the alcohol has been rectified the deeper becomes the tint. The apparatus for measuring the transparency of the liquid (Fig. 58) consists of ten color glasses, varying in color according to the degree of purity of the alcohol. These serve for types of comparison for the tests. The test is conducted as follows: 10 c. c. of alcohol are

FIG. 57.—TEST OF ALCOHOL BY HEAT.

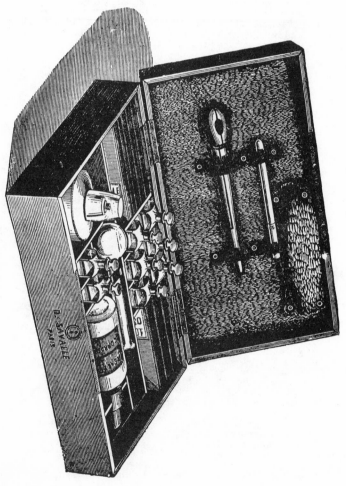

FIG. 58.—DIAPHANOMETER OF SAVALLE.

placed in a small flask and an equal quantity of sulphuric acid (c. p.) is added. The mixture is shaken and heated to boiling (Fig. 57). The source of heat is then removed and the liquid is poured into a white glass flask or test tube and a comparison is made with the test glasses. By this comparison the degree of the impurity can be told at a glance.

The test for aldehyde is made with bisulphite of rosaniline, which is prepared in the following way :

Solution of fuchsine, 1-100 .... 125 c. c.
Solution of sodium bisulphite at 30°.. 75 c. c.
Solution of sulphuric acid, 1-10 ...... 250 c. c.
Water, q. s. to make the volume..... 1 l.

When a certain quantity of the reagent is added to the alcohol, after some minutes a violet red coloration will be seen, varying with the quantity of the aldehyde. Absolute alcohol gives no color. An ammoniacal solution of silver nitrate can also be used, which will be reduced in the presence of the aldehydes.

SECTION II.—BRANDY.

The analysis of brandy comprises : 1, the amount of alcohol ; 2, the amount of extract ; 3, the amount of acidity ; 4, adulterations.

1. Amount of Alcohol.—This cannot be determined directly, as with alcohol, for the brandy is often charged with extractive matter obtained from the vessel in which it is preserved or added to render it proper for consumption. It is necessary to redistill to separate the alcohol. The brandy is diluted with its volume of water and is distilled in the apparatus of Salleron (Fig. 59), which receives the liquid which is condensed in a gauged vessel, and the operation of the still is stopped when the volume of distilled liquid has attained the half of the liquid which was submitted to trial. The strength can then be taken as directed for alcohol.

2. Amount of Extract.—The quantity of extract contained in natural brandy is almost nothing. In reality it is composed of the materials which the alcohol in the brandy may have dissolved in the vessels in which it has been preserved, for in general brandy is kept in casks, so that tannin and some saline materials are fre-

quently found. The amount of extractive matter is
determined in the following manner :
A known quantity of brandy is placed in a capsule
of platinum, glass or porcelain. The capsule is placed
on a stove heated to 100° or above in a water bath, the
desiccation is prolonged until the volatile matter has
been driven off, when the capsule is weighed and the
amount of extractive matter per 100 c. c. (or more often
a liter) is easily determined.

3. Amount of Acidity.—The amount of acidity of
brandy is of prime importance, in view of the appre-

Fig. 59.—STILL OF SALLERON.

ciation of the quality of brandy, which is assured if the
liquor is prepared from a wine of good mixture, without having been submitted to acetic fermentation.
The operation is very simple. In a trial glass place a
known volume of brandy, 10 c. c. for example, with
four or five times its volume of distilled water, and
determine the acidity by means of a solution of potassium, using phthalein, phenol or litmus as indicator.
Acidity is expressed in general in analyses by sulphuric
acid.

4. Examination for Adulterations.—A large part of
the 85° (Gay-Lussac) is consumed under the name of

brandy, from wine, cognac, rum, kirsch, etc., after having been diluted with water and by the addition of various aromatic substances known under the name of sauces or bouquets, added to give a little perfume to the natural product.   Brandy thus prepared is colored with caramel or cachou.

The natural products are themselves submitted to certain operations which have for their end the aging of the product.   One method is to add a few drops of ammonia to each liter or a few grammes of sugar.   The tasting of brandy by a taster who has had long experience is the best means of determining the value of brandy.   Alcohol made from amylaceous materials, beets, potatoes, etc., often contains, by reason of incomplete rectification, alcohols homologous with alcohol from wine.   Separate and mix the suspected alcohol with its volume of ether, then twice its volume of water.   The ether then separates, carrying the foreign alcohols, which can be determined after the slow evaporation of the solvent.   This method of procedure permits the amyl alcohol to be saved.

For methyl alcohol different methods must be employed, the most simple being that of MM. Cazeneuve and Cosson, which shows that impure methyl alcohol is instantly decolorized by potassium permanganate, while ethyl alcohol is only reduced at the end of a long time.   The brandy is distilled to remove the sugar and the caramel, which equally reduces the permanganate of potassium.   The first tenth part which is distilled is used for the test with the permanganate.

M. Reynolds recommends the following process : In the distilled alcohol, which has been brought up to about 50 per cent., a few drops of a weak solution of bichloride of mercury is added and then an excess of potassium in pure ethyl alcohol.   The precipitate is yellow and flocculent.   If the alcohol contains only 10 per cent. of methyl alcohol, the precipitate will be white and not a great deal of it.   This precipitate is dissolved by heat.

SECTION III.—SWEET LIQUORS.

The analysis of liquors comprises :

1. The Amount of Alcohol.—This is determined in the same manner as directed for brandy.

2. Amount of Sugar.—This test is easily made by

means of the cupro-potassium solution of Fehling.* To make the test take exactly 10 c. c. of the solution, add 90 c. c. of water. Then transform the cane sugar to inverted sugar by heating over water bath with 10 per cent. of hydrochloric acid. The inversion requires about a quarter of an hour.

When the liquid is cold it is brought up to its original volume with water. It is then treated with animal black to decolorize it. After some hours of repose, filter. The liquid, after filtering, should be perfectly colorless. Dilute anew and test for the total amount of sugar contained in the sample.

To test for sugar, put in a capsule of porcelain or in a flask an exactly measured quantity of the Fehling solution. Then, after having diluted it, the mixture is carried to the boiling point, the liquid is let fall drop by drop, with the aid of a burette divided (Figs. 60 and 61) into tenths of a cubic centimeter, into the sugar. The liquid is decolorized and diluted until the copper is completely precipitated in the form of red oxide of copper. The end of the operation is indicated by the complete decolorization of the top layer, which now has the look of pure water. If it preserves a blue tint, the reduction is not finished; if, on the other hand, the liquid becomes yellow, an excess of sugar must have been used, as the tint is due to the action of the potassium on the sugar.

3. Test for Glucose and Dextrine.—Glucose is found normally in liquors called fancy, and in this case is perfectly legitimate, but a large number of liquor manufacturers also employ dextrine (British gum) in their liquors, it is said, to make them more mellow. This practice is bad, commercial glucose being rarely pure enough, and it gives to liquors a distinctive taste of its own.

The presence of glucose in liquors is determined in the following manner. The amount of sugar before and after inversion is determined. The first operation gives us a quantity of naturally inverted sugar existing in solution always very weak in liquors prepared with the juice of fruits, and the glucose which may have

---

* Sulphate of copper cryst.....   34.639 grms. in 500 c. c. of water.
  Rochelle salts.............. ...173   "   " 400 "   "
  Sodic hydrate.................50   "   " 100 "   "

Keep the sulphate of copper solution in one flask, the other in another. Mix as wanted for use.

been added. The second test gives the total amount of sugar. If the quantity of sugar which reduces the liquor of Fehling without previous inversion is con-

FIG. 60.—BURETTE.

FIG. 61.—BURETTE.

siderable, relative to the total quantity of sugar, the presence of sugar is certain. This can be determined by the polariscope.

In a polariscope tube of 22 centimeters various liquors

FIG. 62.—DRUM OF DIALYZER.

which have served in the test of sugars are successively introduced. If the two liquors deflect the ray of polarized light to the right, the presence of glucose is assured, for the sugar deviates constantly to the right with polarized light, while the sugar which has been inverted and the sugar of fruits give a deviation to the left. The general method of determining the different elements which enter into a mixture of sugars will be given farther on in treating of the analysis of simple sirups.

Dextrine is also easy to determine by a process called dialysis, founded on the property possessed by sugars of passing through membranes, such as parchment, etc., while dextrine is retained by it.

In the drum of a dialyzer (Fig. 62) place a sufficient quantity of liquid, say 100 to 200 c. c., and the instrument is placed in a vessel as represented in Fig. 63, the

FIG. 63.—DIALYZER.

water in the vessel being constantly renewed. After some days, when all trace of sugar has disappeared, the liquid of the dialyzer is concentrated over a water bath to a sirupy consistence.

The sirup is then thrown in two or three times its volume of absolute alcohol, which precipitates the dextrine in the form of white flocculent matter. This is gathered on a filter, washed several times with alcohol and is dissolved with the aid of heat. This solution then serves for a trial solution for testing for dextrine. With the polariscope the light turns to the right. The presence of dextrine in small quantity in a liquor is generally the indication of the presence of glucose. This sugar is nearly always present, above all in liquors prepared from amylaceous materials saccharified by diastase.

Another indication of the employment of glucose is furnished by the presence of calcium sulphate in liquors, which is employed to saturate the excess of sulphuric acid which served to saccharify the first materials.

The presence of salt in the ash is determined by the calcination of the extractive matter of liquors. The mineral matter so obtained is dissolved in weak hydrochloric acid, and is then treated with barium chloride; if a precipitate is the result, the presence of the sulphate will be proved.

4. Examination for Saccharine.—This is treated in speaking of the analysis of sirups farther on.

5. Examination for Essences and their Approximate Amount.—A large amount of the essences contained in a liquor can be extracted in the following manner: A sufficient quantity of liquor, say 100 c. c., for example, is diluted with its volume of water, or with one and one-half times its volume, according to its alcoholic strength. The solution is agitated with ether in a decantation beaker. When, after repose, the solvent is separated by decantation, the ethereal solution is filtered and allowed to freely evaporate, or is placed in a vacuum. The extract which is obtained is composed of essences taken from the liquor by the ether, which permits of its value being estimated. If the operation has been made with exactly measured volumes, the weight of the extract obtained by the evaporation of the ether in the vacuum gives very approximately, it is true, the total quantity of essences which were used in the preparation of the liquor which was analyzed.

6. Examination for Coloring Matters.—As has already been seen, a certain number of coloring materials are permitted in the preparation of liquors. The

examination for injurious colors, especially the anilines, is more in the province of the chemist than in that of the liquor manufacturers.

7. Liquors which Contain no Sugar.—The analysis of liquors which contain no sugar, as absinthe, is done in the same manner as of those which contain sugar. Its chief interest rests in determining the amount of the extractive matter, which determines whether the liquor was made by means of essences or infusions.

CHAPTER II.

ANALYSIS OF SUGAR AND SIRUPS.

FOR determining sugar three methods may be employed :

1. That of Fehling.
2. By means of the specific gravity.
3. By the optical method.

1. The first method has already been described.
2. This method is only applicable to solutions of pure sugar. The density is determined by means of

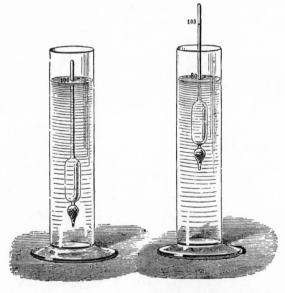

In Pure Water.   In a liquid of 1·25 Specific Gravity.

FIGS. 64 AND 65.—HYDROMETERS FOR LIQUIDS HEAVIER THAN WATER.

the areometer, which is called in this case the sac-charometer (Figs. 64 and 65); this gives directly the strength.   When the ordinary areometer is used, special tables must be used to give the result.

3.   Estimation of Sugar by Means of the Optical Method.—This method is founded on the action of solutions of sugar on polarized light, which is meas-ured by means of the polariscope, and for full infor-mation on this subject the reader is referred to Tuck-er's or Weichmann's works on sugar analysis.

THE END

APPENDIX.

UNITED STATES STANDARD WEIGHTS AND MEASURES.

The following tables have been issued from the Office of Standard Weights and Measures, United States Coast and Geodetic Survey, T. C. Mendenhall, Superintendent.

TABLES FOR CONVERTING UNITED STATES WEIGHTS AND MEASURES—
CUSTOMARY TO METRIC.

1. *Linear.*

	Inches to Millimeters.	Feet to Meters	Yards to Meters.	Miles to Kilometers.
1 =	25·4000	0·304801	0·914402	1·60935
2 =	50 8001	0·609601	1·828804	3·21869
3 =	76·2001	0·914402	2·743205	4·82804
4 =	101·6002	1·219202	3·657607	6·43739
5 =	127·0002	1·524003	4·572009	8·04674
6 =	152·4003	1·828804	5·486411	9·65608
7 =	177·8003	2·133604	6·400813	11·26543
8 =	203·2004	2·438405	7·315215	12·87478
9 =	228·6004	2·743205	8·229616	14·48412

2. *Square.*

	Square Inches to Square Centimeters.	Square Feet to Square Decimeters.	Square Yards to Square Meters.	Acres to Hectares.
1 =	6·452	9·290	0·836	0·4047
2 =	12·903	18·581	1·672	0·8094
3 =	19·355	27·871	2·508	1·2141
4 =	25·807	37·161	3·344	1·6187
5 =	32·258	46·452	4·181	2·0234
6 =	38·710	55·742	5·017	2 4281
7 =	45·161	65·032	5·853	2·8328
8 =	51·613	74·323	6·689	3 2375
9 =	58 065	83·613	7·525	3·6422

3. *Cubic.*

	Cubic Inches to Cubic Centimeters.	Cubic Feet to Cubic Meters.	Cubic Yards to Cubic Meters.	Bushels to Hectoliters.
1 =	16·387	0·02832	0·765	0·35242
2 =	32·774	0·05663	1·529	0·70485
3 =	49·161	0·08495	2·294	1·05727
4 =	65·549	0·11327	3·058	1·40969
5 =	81·936	0·14158	3·823	1·76211
6 =	98·323	0·16990	4·587	2·11454
7 =	114·710	0·19822	5·352	2·46696
8 =	131·097	0·22654	6·116	2·81938
9 =	147·484	0·25485	6·881	3·17181

4. *Capacity.*

	Fluid Drachms to Milliliters or Cubic Centimeters.	Fluid Ounces to Milliliters.	Quarts to Liters.	Gallons to Liters.
1 =	3·70	29·57	0·94636	3·78544
2 =	7·39	59·15	1·89272	7·57088
3 =	11·09	88·72	2·83908	11·35632
4 =	14·79	118·30	3·78544	15·14176
5 =	18·48	147·87	4·73180	18·92720
6 =	22·18	177·44	5·67816	22·71264
7 =	25·88	207·02	6·62452	26·49808
8 =	29·57	236·59	7·57088	30·28352
9 =	33·28	266·16	8·51724	34·06896

5. *Weight.*

	Grains to Milligrams.	Avoirdupois Ounces to Grams.	Avoirdupois Pounds to Kilograms.	Troy Ounces to Grams.
1 =	64·7989	28·3495	0·45359	31·10348
2 =	129·5978	56·6991	0·90719	62·20696
3 =	194·3968	85·0486	1·36078	93·31044
4 =	259·1957	113·3981	1·81437	124·41392
5 =	323·9946	141·7476	2·26796	155·51740
6 =	388·7935	170·0972	2·72156	186·62089
7 =	453·5924	198·4467	3·17515	217·72437
8 =	518·3914	226·7962	3·62874	248·82785
9 =	583·1903	255·1457	4·08233	279·93133

6. *Miscellaneous.*

1 chain	=	20·1169	meters.
1 square mile	=	259	hectares.
1 fathom	=	1·829	meters.
1 nautical mile	=	1853·27	meters.
1 foot = 0·304801 meter,		9·4840158	log.
1 avoirdupois pound	=	453·5924277	grams.
15432·35639 grains	=	1	kilogram.

TABLES FOR CONVERTING UNITED STATES WEIGHTS AND MEASURES—
METRIC TO CUSTOMARY.

7. *Linear.*

	Meters to Inches.	Meters to Feet.	Meters to Yards.	Kilometers to Miles.
1 =	39·3700	3·28083	1·093611	0·62137
2 =	78·7400	6·56167	2·187222	1·24274
3 =	118·1100	9·84250	3·280833	1·86411
4 =	157·4800	13·12333	4·374444	2·48548
5 =	196·8500	16·40417	5·468056	3·10685
6 =	236·2200	19·68500	6·561667	3·72822
7 =	275·5900	22·96583	7·655278	4·34959
8 =	314·9600	26·24667	8·748889	4·97096
9 =	354·3300	29·52750	9·842500	5·59233

8. *Square.*

	Square Centimeters to Square Inches.	Square Meters to Square Feet.	Square Meters to Square Yards.	Hectares to Acres.
1 =	0·1550	10·764	1·196	2·471
2 =	0·3100	21·528	2·392	4·942
3 =	0·4650	32·292	3·588	7·413
4 =	0·6200	43·055	4·784	9·884
5 =	0·7750	53·819	5·980	12·355
6 =	0·9300	64·583	7·176	14·826
7 =	1·0850	75·347	8·372	17·297
8 =	1·2400	86·111	9·568	19·768
9 =	1·3950	96·874	10·764	22·239

9. *Cubic.*

	Cubic Centimeters to Cubic Inches.	Cubic Decimeters to Cubic Inches.	Cubic Meters to Cubic Feet.	Cubic Meters to Cubic Yards.
1 =	0·0610	61·023	35·314	1·308
2 =	0·1220	122·047	70·629	2 616
3 =	0·1831	183·070	105·943	3·924
4 =	0·2441	244 093	141·258	5·232
5 =	0·3051	305·117	176·572	6·540
6 =	0 3661	366·140	211·887	7·848
7 =	0·4272	427·163	247·201	9·156
8 =	0·4882	488 187	282·516	10·464
9 =	0·5492	549·210	317·830	11·771

10. *Capacity.*

	Milliliters or Cubic Centiliters to Fluid Drachms.	Centiliters to Fluid Ounces.	Liters to Quarts.	Dekaliters to Gallons.	Hectoliters to Bushels.
1 =	0·27	0·338	1·0567	2·6417	2·8375
2 =	0·54	0·676	2·1134	5·2834	5·6750
3 =	0·81	1·014	3·1700	7·9251	8·5125
4 =	1 08	1·352	4·2267	10·5668	11·3500
5 =	1·35	1·691	5·2834	13·2085	14·1875
6 =	1·62	2·029	6·3401	15·8502	17·0250
7 =	1·89	2·368	7·3968	18 4919	19·8625
8 =	2·16	2·706	8·4534	21·1336	22 7000
9 =	2·43	3·043	9·5101	23·7753	25·5375

11. *Weight.*

	Milligrams to Grains.	Kilograms to Grains.	Hectograms (100 Grm.) to Ounces Avoirdupois.	Kilograms to Pounds Avoirdupois.
1 =	0·01543	15432·36	3 5274	2·20462
2 =	0·03086	30864·71	7·0548	4·40924
3 =	0·04630	46297·07	10 5822	6·61386
4 =	0·06173	61729·43	14 1096	8·81849
5 =	0·07716	77161·78	17·6370	11·02311
6 =	0·09259	92594·14	21·1644	13·22773
7 =	0·10803	108026 49	24 6918	15 43235
8 =	0·12346	123458·85	28·2192	17·63697
9 =	0·13889	138891·21	31 7466	19 84159

12. *Weight—(continued.)*

	Quintals to Pounds Avoirdupois.	Milliers or Tonnes to Pounds Avoirdupois.	Grams to Ounces Troy.
1 =	220·46	2204·6	0·03215
2 =	440·92	4409·2	0·06430
3 =	661 38	6613·8	0·09645
4 =	881·84	8818·4	0·12860
5 =	1102·30	11023·0	0·16075
6 =	1322·76	13227·6	0·19290
7 =	1543·22	15432·2	0·22505
8 =	1763·68	17636·8	0·25721
9 =	1984·14	19841·4	0·28936

The only authorized material standard of customary length is the Troughton scale belonging to this office, whose length at 59·62° Fah. conforms to the British standard. The yard in use in the United States is, therefore, equal to the British yard.

The only authorized material standard of customary weight is the troy pound of the mint. It is of brass of unknown density, and, therefore, not suitable for a standard of mass. It was derived from the British standard troy pound of 1758 by direct comparison. The British avoirdupois pound was also derived from the latter, and contains 7,000 grains troy.

The grain troy is, therefore, the same as the grain avoirdupois, and the pound avoirdupois in use in the United States is equal to the British pound avoirdupois.

The British gallon = 4·54346 liters.

The British bushel = 36·3477 liters.

By the concurrent action of the principal governments of the world, an International Bureau of Weights and Measures has been established near Paris. Under the direction of the International Committee, two ingots were cast of pure platinum-iridium in the proportion of 9 parts of the former to 1 part of the latter metal. From one of these a certain number of kilogrammes were prepared, from the other a definite number of meter bars. These standards of weight and length were intercompared, without preference, and certain ones were selected as international prototype standards. The others were distributed by lot to the different governments, and are called national prototype standards. Those apportioned to the United States are in the keeping of this office.

The metric system was legalized in the United States in 1866.

The international standard meter is derived from the *metre des archives*, and its length is defined by the distance between two lines at 0° Centigrade, on a platinum-iridium bar deposited at the International Bureau of Weights and Measures.

The international standard kilogramme is a mass of platinum-iridium deposited at the same place, and its weight in vacuo is the same as that of the kilogramme des archives.

The liter is equal to a cubic decimeter of water, and it is measured by the quantity of distilled water which, at its maximum density, will counterpoise the standard kilogramme in a vacuum, the volume of such a quantity of water being, as nearly as has been ascertained, equal to a cubic decimeter.

THERMOMETER SCALES.

MUCH annoyance is caused by the great difference of thermometer scales in use in the different civilized countries. The scale of Reamur prevails in Germany. As is well known, he divides the space between the freezing and boiling points into 80°. France uses the centigrade scale, graduated on the decimal system. The most peculiar scale of all, however, is that of Fahrenheit, a renowned German physicist, who, in 1714 or 1715, composed his scale, having ascertained that water can be cooled under the freezing point, without congealing. He therefore did not take the congealing point of water, which is uncertain, but composed a mixture of equal parts of snow and sal ammonic, about 14° R. This scale is preferable to both those of Reaumur and Celesius, or, as it is also called, centigrade, because : 1. The regular temperatures of the moderate zone move within its two zeros, and can therefore be written without + or —. 2. The scale is divided so finely that it is not necessary to use fractions whenever careful observations are to be made. These advantages, although drawn into question by some, have been considered sufficiently weighty that both Great Britain and America have retained the scales, while the nations of the Continent, France, Spain, etc., use the other two.

To change a temperature as given by Fahrenheit's scale into the same as given by the centigrade scale, subtract 32 from Fahrenheit's degrees, and multiply the remainder by $\frac{5}{9}$. The product will be the temperature in centigrade degrees.

To change from Fahrenheit's to Reaumur's scale, subtract 32 from Fahrenheit's degrees, and multiply the remainder by $\frac{4}{9}$. The product will be the temperature in Reaumur's degrees.

To change the temperature as given by the centigrade scale into the same as given by Fahrenheit, multiply the centigrade degrees by $\frac{9}{5}$ and add 32° to the product. The sum will be the temperature by Fahrenheit's scale.

To change from Reaumur's to Fahrenheit's scale, multiply the degrees on Reaumur's scale by $\frac{9}{4}$, and add 32° to the product. The sum will be the temperature by Fahrenheit's scale.

INDEX.

196   INDEX.